Nashua

Nashua

by EDWARD L. BOWEN

THOROUGHBRED
Legends®
No. 8

EP
ECLIPSE
PRESS

Lexington, Kentucky

Library of Congress Card Number: 00-104792

ISBN 1-58150-050-5

Printed in The United States
First Edition: March 2001

a division of
The Blood-Horse, Inc.
PUBLISHERS SINCE 1916

ECLIPSE
PRESS

To learn more about Nashua
and other classic Thoroughbreds, see:

www.thoroughbredlegends.com

NASHUA

CONTENTS

NASHUA

INTRODUCTION

Getting His Irish Up

"Grahb the harse, Clem! Grahb the harse!"

Young Clem Florio had regarded the huge, friendly Joe McGrath, with his Irish brogue, as something of a mentor in the Fitzsimmons stable. He was at a loss, however, as to why the big Irishman was peering beneath those bushy eyebrows and speaking with such urgency.

"The harse" was a husky colt being led off a van at Sunny Jim Fitzsimmons' barn at Aqueduct. McGrath was urging the young groom to step forward and take the colt from the fellow leading him off the van. First guy to the shank, perhaps, gets to be his groom.

Sunny Jim Fitzsimmons was widely recognized as a legendary horse trainer in Thoroughbred racing, a status he had earned long ago with hardscuffle survival and high-class success. He had reached octogenarian status, and over the years arthritis had folded down his spine so punishingly that he had to look up at the withers of a well-grown racehorse. He could not be said to be a lonely old man, since several of his sons had been his assistants and his cavalry of grandchildren was getting past name-recollection numbers. Still, Fitzsimmons could be assumed to be near the end of his career. Certainly, life's changes had circled him with their unrelenting finality.

His wife of sixty years had passed away barely three years earlier, ending his life's adventure with the former Jenny Harvey, the young New Jersey girl who had signed on for the uncertainties of a racetrack existence in 1891. Then, too, grand old William Woodward Sr. had died just months before. To be sure, it was good news that a son, William Jr., had decided to maintain his father's proud Belair Stud and Stable, and, of course, Fitz's other enduring patron, the Wheatley Stable of the Phipps family, was still in good shape. Nevertheless, the death of the old gent he had called "W. W.," who had sent him winners of ten classic races, including two Triple Crowns, surely seemed to whisper "end of an era."

Ah, but coming down the ramp was what Fitzsimmons recognized as "the Segula colt," a fetching mahogany bay with a white star. Of all the princelings that the Woodward stable had sent to him or to its English stable, perhaps none suggested more eloquently a taste of tomorrows, not yesterdays. Indeed, that haphazard balm that Thoroughbred racing can supply its mortal supplicants like few other endeavors was poised to slather its goodness on the Fitzsimmons stable. At a stage in life when retirement and fading memories seemed to lurk around the shedrow, Sunny Jim Fitzsimmons was about to embark on some of his greatest years.

"The Segula colt" was none other than the future champion Nashua, while other two-year-olds in the stable that year were Wheatley's champion-to-be fillies High Voltage and Misty Morn. And, by the time these had left the track, another crack runner in the Wheatley silks had already arrived on the scene, justifying the inherent potency of his name — Bold Ruler.

When Nashua was settled into one of the stalls assigned Clem Florio at the Aqueduct racetrack, all of American sport had been predestined to a whirlwind of emotion. Ahead lay spectacular victories and disheartening defeats, an all-time earnings title, television stardom, a rivalry with Swaps that was the stuff of national news, a stunning Society death that has never lost its power of sensationalism, and the most famous horse auction of all time.

"Grahb the harse, Clem! Grahb the harse!"

Why? What made Joe McGrath so adamant, the bewildered young Florio had to ask. There was imagery, and guile, to the answer.

"The old man tried to straighten up when he saw him!"

Edward L. Bowen
Lexington, Kentucky, 2000

NASHUA

CHAPTER I

A Prince In The Offing

The husky bay colt was, indeed, delivered into the care of young Clem Florio, the former groom recalls with pride today. It would be a short, happy partnership. The son of Nasrullah—Segula had been earmarked for one of breeder Woodward Sr.'s annual shipment of yearlings to England, but the breeder had died and his son had decided that taking over an American racing string was quite enough. It did not take long for the whole stable to recognize that old Mr. Woodward had picked the colt out as potentially special for good reason.

A few seasons with the Fitzsimmons stable was a transition phase in the life of Clem Florio. They came after his less-than-championship boxing career. "It was a natural thing to go to the racetrack," he recalls now, many years later, after having settled into a successful career as a racing writer in Baltimore.

Boxing had given him an odd introduction to racing, and to Mr. Fitzsimmons.

"I lived so close to Aqueduct that I would slip under the fence and do my running right on the track," Florio says, with perhaps some wonder at his own youthful brashness. "When I went to ask the old man for a job, he said, 'You're the fellow who scared my horses with that towel.' It was true; I used to wear a towel around my neck when I was training."

Fast forward to the advanced stages of Nashua's conditioning, and we shall see this personal experience with the footing of the old Aqueduct track turns out to have created a handicapper's edge.

A fellow named Fitzsimmons in the racing game might be expected to have a brace of Irish names around him, and, in addition to Joe McGrath, Sunny Jim's staff included Bart Sweeney and a key exercise rider named Bill McCleary. One of the journeyman riders who rode some of the stable horses — although rarely the stars — and who worked them in the mornings was one Jess Higley.

A fellow named Clem Florio does not figure to be Irish, not totally, anyway, and this one was not. Nor was his friend Louie, whom he brought around with him and with whom he worked a double-duty schedule to allow each an extra day off. Florio was green, but smart enough to pay attention to the Irish lads — "they came to the stall to sniff around" — and saw that they clearly had a glint in the eye over Nashua.

"One morning, Higley came to the barn," Florio said recently, the sequence as vivid after more than forty years as one's first date, or bout (should they be different occasions). "He said they were going to 'do something with the horse today.' I could tell he had his whip stuck up the back of his jacket."

Florio turned the horse over to the lead pony rider and dashed for the rail. Fitzsimmons on occasion would work as many as four or five young horses together, he explained, and on this day Nashua was parked on the outside:

"I had run on that part of the track, and I knew how deep it was out there. I had my watch, and I got him in :47 2/5 (for a half-mile)!"

He later teased the Irish fellows that he had told all his Italian friends.

"Now, Clem, why would you do a thing like that?" they asked.

He confessed; he had kept his mouth as tightly sealed as they had.

It was soon time for Nashua's debut, which came on May 5, 1954, at nearby Belmont Park. Florio thinks he was probably making $65 a week; he bet $60 on Nashua.

The colt was not as well talked up around the track as might be presumed after stablemate Dark Ruler's victorious debut two days earlier. Perhaps Fitzsimmons' reputation for running horses hard created a scent of racing a big, rawboned colt into shape rather than having him strung tight first time out. Florio and the lads were treated to odds of 8 1/2-1, even though Nashua was in a three-horse entry with Belair's Anacostia and Wheatley's Out of Reach.

Higley was on Nashua for a four and a half-furlong dash down the Widener Chute, which cut across the track at Belmont Park. As was common on that straight course, a huge field, twenty-one maiden juveniles, turned out. Higley had Nashua in about the top third of the tightly packed field early, and in the final three-sixteenths, the colt ran away to win by three lengths. The time was :52 3/5. "They knew they had a killer," was Florio's pronouncement.

Eddie Arcaro, mid-pack on a colt named Golden Prince, was impressed by the pistonlike haunches he saw leaving him in the dust. The following year, in a report for *Sports Illustrated*, Arcaro recalled of that maiden race: "I still have a vivid recollection of Nashua turning on a wonderful burst of speed and winning easily by three lengths...I have had such a 'second sense' — about horses before this — with Assault and Citation, for instance. In Nashua's case I knew instinctively as he drew away from his field that this was a horse with a determined will to win."

Higley would not be around for the second start. Likewise, Fitzsimmons moved Nashua away from Clem and Louie, as Florio recalls, and turned him over to the more experienced Alfred Robertson, a former rider.

Robertson and colt were together for the rest of Nashua's career. That career continued in earnest a week after the debut, when Nashua skipped up to stakes class for the five-furlong Juvenile Stakes at Belmont Park. Arcaro, the most famous rider of the day, had come calling, so it was he who was adorned in the historic Belair Stud colors of white with red polka dots and red cap.

Two great rivalries added extra interest to Nashua's career, the first of which began that day. Mrs. R. A. Firestone (later Mrs. John W. Galbreath) and trainer Sherrill Ward had unleashed another of the young strutters in the classy two-year-old division in New York — a lean, racy Heliopolis colt named Summer Tan. This one already had stakes experience, having taken the Youthful Stakes in late April, and conditions in the Juvenile had him giving five pounds to Nashua.

Fitzsimmons also started another colt, Wheatley Stable's Laugh — who had placed in each of his two starts — and the entry was 3-1 as third choice. Greentree Stable also had an impressive early winner named Gold Box in the race, and he was a slight favorite, even over Summer Tan.

Arcaro had Nashua on the lead from the start, and they dashed the first quarter-mile in :22 1/5. Summer Tan and Eric Guerin then came along and, according to the inexact science of a chartcaller peering diagonally up a chute, got a half-length in front. Summer Tan was credited with the half-mile in :45 3/5. Nashua felt the Arcaro whip for the first time, but not fiercely, and he rallied to regain the edge and won by a half-length. The

15

time was :58. Laugh was third, eight lengths behind, with Gold Box fourth in a field of eight. Guerin took another crack at victory, claiming that the winner had been at fault when the pair brushed at the furlong pole, but the stewards allowed the finish order to stand.

So, Sunny Jim Fitzsimmons had another budding star. At the same time, Wheatley Stable's High Voltage had established a similar impression in the juvenile filly division. Fitzsimmons had been training this sort of high-class horse for high-class stables for three decades, but that length of time accounted for less than half of his career on the racetrack.

James E. Fitzsimmons was born in 1874 in a house that, prophetically, was on land that five years later was transformed into the Coney Island Jockey Club's showy Sheepshead Bay track on Long Island. Fitzsimmons was not quite eleven when he got a job around the race-track, doing stable and kitchen chores in the summer for the Brennan Brothers at the new track.

He later began working full time for the famed Dwyer Brothers' stable and presumably got his first familiarity with a great three-year-old. The year was 1887, when Mike and Phil Dwyer's magnificent

Hanover thundered to twenty victories from twenty-seven races.

When he was about fifteen, Fitzsimmons arrived back at the stable at Brighton Beach one afternoon and was asked by Hardy Campbell, who had a division of the Dwyer horses, if he could ride a race. With little fanfare but plenty of butterflies, he made his debut on a horse named Newburgh, finishing fourth.

Rides for the Dwyers were not frequent, and the competition was fierce. Fitzsimmons accepted reality and headed for the outlaw tracks.

George F. T. Ryall, who wrote gracefully of racing for *New Yorker* magazine for many years under the name Audax Minor, penned a two-part series on Fitzsimmons for *The Blood-Horse* in 1963. Ryall noted that Fitzsimmons first was tagged "Sunny Jim" by *New York World* sports editor George Dailey, who was borrowing the name of a likeable cartoon character of his day.

Ryall helped put into perspective what the racing world was like in the early days for his old pal: "Outlaw tracks were thicker than blackberries, and Mr. Fitz had a go at all of them. 'No matter where there was racing, I was there,' he says."

There was little concept of authority in racing in those days, so exactly what made one track an outlaw track and another a "legit" track might have been to some extent in the eye of the beholder. Still, the places where Fitzsimmons scuffled were on the shady side.

Ryall reeled off such names as Gloucester and Guttenburg in New Jersey, Maspeth on Long Island, Saint Asaph and Alexander Island in Virginia, Elkton, Marcus Hook, and Sunny Side in Maryland, Barksdale and Carnegie in Pennsylvania. Even old Aqueduct was an outlaw track when it opened in 1894. Fitzsimmons rode at them all.

This was not all seasonal stuff. In the last three decades of the 20th century, winter racing and night racing in the Northeast might have been regarded as unseemly intrusions into the glories of the sport. Well, they had both been tried about a century before, and Fitzsimmons had been there to ride. This was all in a day when distances of fifty miles or less between race-tracks were commonly traversed by leading a horse on foot; for long treks, freight cars could do the job.

For all the leaky roof and loose rule image of such racing, however, Fitzsimmons told Ryall years later that he only twice was asked to tinker with the results of a race. Still, riding horses, some of which he trained, or owned, in that echelon was not so glamorous, especially for a fellow who had become a married man at the age of seventeen. Any chance at a score was precious, so much so that Fitzsimmons once sweated off eleven pounds in a day for a chance to make $100 for a ride. Fitzsimmons had rigged up a homemade sweat box, and also shoveled clay at a brickyard to help sweat off pounds. Ryall reported that he not only made the weight, "but despite being pretty shaky, won the race."

By the late 1890s, Fitzsimmons despaired of the future and was ready to accept a job with the Philadelphia street railway. But only a few days before he was to report, he heard that a Main Line type named Col. Edward de V. Morrell was looking for a trainer. Fitzsimmons leapt at the chance, and, given the social status of his patron-to-be, was granted a license — a ticket punched "legitimate"— by The Jockey Club, which had been created in 1894.

Fitz trained for Morrell for about five years, and he was leading trainer at Pimlico in 1904. Two years later, he left to start a public stable headquartered at Aqueduct.

Pristine this was not, for several of his patrons were pretty well up in the Tammany Hall scheme of things.

When New York racing was blacked out by anti-gambling legislation, Fitzsimmons was forced onto the road again, racing in Maryland and Canada. After a couple of seasons, racing in New York was revived. The hunt clubs devised a plan to purchase drafts of two-year-olds in Kentucky, where the market was depressed, and parcel them out to members. Fitzsimmons noted that these well-heeled, respectable sportsmen suddenly had horses, but no trainer, and he dove to their rescue. Sunny Jim suddenly was a class act.

Fitzsimmons' stable of clients increased, and by 1915, Ryall noted, he won fifty-one races and $27,890 in prize money for the season. In 1917, he became the trainer for the Quincy Stable of James F. Johnson. By the early 1920s, the string there numbered fifty horses, one of the largest in the country, and was split among several trainers. Even so, there was no escaping the shadow of controversy. Johnson had purchased Playfellow, a younger full brother to Man o' War (who had not yet started). The year after Man o' War's retirement, Playfellow came to hand, and he won a couple of

races in impressive fashion, three days apart. Coupled with the glamour of his full brother, this made him so hot an item that Harry Sinclair bought him for $100,000 in his ambitious plans for Rancocas Stable.

After Playfellow lost his next two races, one in which the new owner was said to have bet enough to recoup his purchase price, Sinclair supposedly found the horse to be a cribber and a windsucker. He cried foul and sued. One trial ended in a deadlock, a second found in favor of Sinclair, abetted by testimony from parties only obliquely connected to the horse. Fitzsimmons was later quoted with expected indignation, pointing out correctly that the horse had come off consecutive victories and clearly had no condition that compromised his ability to do so. Johnson's luck, having turned bad, stayed bad, and he became discouraged about the game in general.

At what seemed a dark hour, Fitzsimmons got an offer in 1923 to train for William Woodward Sr., and he took it forthwith. At last, the long struggles with indifferent horses, shaky tracks, and shakier stables were over. The promised land had come calling, and Belair was its name.

CHAPTER 2

Champions And Challenges

S unny Jim Fitzsimmons had a reputation for being hard on horses. The translation has always been that he trained horses vigorously and raced them often, rather than any hint of abusing them. In his 1963 article, George Ryall cut right to the heart of the matter:

"...training methods have always been divided into two distinct schools, the severe and the lenient, towards which individual trainers veer one way or another. Because it was the one he was brought up in, Mr. Fitz quite naturally inclined to the hard — now called the old-fashioned — way. His horses were freely and often extended in their morning workouts, and if they stood up to their preparation they seldom failed on the race course in the afternoon. Of course, many fell by the wayside before they got that far, but that was to be expected. Provided they are not out of the ordinary in temperament or constitution, race horses adapt themselves to the ways of their trainers. 'But each one is different,' Mr. Fitz says, 'and you've got to watch them for any peculiarities. A horse with bad habits usually finishes second.' "

At the time Nashua was three, Fitzsimmons was quoted, "You know, this training must get very monotonous for a horse. I think it's better to race them into shape and keep them that way. Just galloping every day must wear hard on him. He's got to get bored, and that's not good..."

As is so often the case with good horsemen, however, generalizing about Fitzsimmons' technique is not universally accurate, or fair. True, he raced his first good horse for Belair a Hanover-like twenty-seven times at three, and, true, he ran Seabiscuit thirty-five times at two and twelve more times at three before casting off the future champion. On the other hand, none of the colts with which Fitzsimmons won the Belmont ever raced more than a dozen times at three. Also, one of Fitzsimmons' most acclaimed feats was the opposite of racing a horse into shape, for he brought Nashua back for his successful four-year-old debut off training and a four-month layoff.

Woodward, a distinguished Turfman of Edwardian mien, a New York banker, and an American aristocrat in the best sense of the term, hired Fitzsimmons in the autumn of 1923. Sunny Jim was nearly fifty years old.

The next year was a good one. Priscilla Ruley won ten of her twenty-seven races for them, more than any other high-ranking three-year-old filly won that season, and she defeated the great Princess Doreen in the Alabama Stakes. Priscilla Ruley also won the Gazelle and defeated males in the Jerome. Another Belair star of the year was Aga Khan, winner of the Lawrence Realization.

Two years later, Fitzsimmons was handed another plum of an assignment, when he was invited also to train the fledgling Wheatley Stable of Mrs. Henry Carnegie Phipps and her brother, Ogden Mills. The connection of Fitzsimmons and the Phippses was to last nearly forty years, until the trainer's retirement.

Belair and Wheatley were all about stayers and the classics, but neither Woodward nor Mrs. Phipps failed to understand the importance of speed to balance stamina. The first wave of good horses Fitzsimmons had for Wheatley included a two-year-old whose name and

tragedy must have wafted back into mind as he con-
templated the bristling precocity of the young Nashua.
This was Dice, who in the spring and summer of 1927
dashed off five wins in five races, including the Keene
Memorial, Hudson, Juvenile, and Great American
Stakes. A succulent Saratoga seemed to beckon from
the leafy pungency of upstate New York, but Dice died
there of an internal hemorrhage.

Fitzsimmons regarded Dice as the best horse he had
trained at the time the colt was two, and the loss of the
horse carried a sting of sorrow long afterward.

By 1930, William Woodward Sr.'s participation in
the importation of Sir Gallahad III to the Hancock family's Claiborne Farm (where he kept his mares) came to
full flower in the form of the stallion's son Gallant Fox.
This rakish, big colt swept what would be known as the
Triple Crown — the Kentucky Derby, Preakness, and
Belmont Stakes. In his first crop, Gallant Fox then sired
the next Triple Crown winner, Omaha, and in his second crop he got another Belmont winner and champion, Granville. Mr. Fitz trained them all. Faireno had
won another Belmont for Belair and Fitzsimmons amid
that wave of glory, and then, when the powerful

Johnstown won the Derby and Belmont in 1939, Fitzsimmons had won ten classic races within a decade.

Although Mr. Fitz might have noted that the calendar had been fiddling about with an eightieth birthday, one doubts he spent much time reflecting upon all those past glories as he went about the daily chores of managing Nashua, High Voltage, and others in his stable in the spring of 1954. After Nashua's elevation to the status of stakes winner, in the Juvenile, the husky colt was next sent down to New Jersey, where Garden State Park was inaugurating the $15,000-added Cherry Hill Stakes on May 19. Again, there were only seven days between races, so Nashua was making his third start in as many weeks.

Stable reliable Higley was again in the saddle. Arcaro had been called before arch steward Marshall Cassidy for a riding incident two days before. Arcaro admitted he had been a bit careless, and Cassidy said, "Well, let's go fishing," and handed out a ten-day suspension. (High Voltage won the National Stallion Stakes, filly division, at Belmont on the same day as the Cherry Hill, so it might not have been certain Arcaro would have been on Nashua, anyway.)

Royal Note, who had won the Lafayette Stakes and Bashford Manor Stakes in Kentucky, was the 2-1 choice for the Cherry Hill, with Nashua second favorite at 3-1. The favorite was giving the Belair colt three pounds, 122 to 119, in a field of eleven. Jockey Sammy Boulmetis got Royal Note off to a quick lead and, although Nashua was lapped on him early, the Spy Song colt drew out to daylight and a bit more after three furlongs in the five-furlong test. Nashua closed most of the ground, but was lugging in through the final stages, so that Higley had to split his ambition between getting to the front and keeping his mount off the leader. Royal Note won by a neck in the fast time of :58 3/5, which was just two-fifths of a second over the track record. Beaten for the first time, Nashua was five lengths ahead of the third-place finisher, the filly Menolene (who within a couple of years would be known as the half-sister to Needles). This time it was Nashua's rider who took a flyer on the stewards, seeing culpability in the winner, but the impression from on high was that Nashua was more at fault for the jostling than the other colt.

Nashua was not seen again under colors for three

months. The important, traditional Saratoga races were his targets, leading to the big autumn tests. On August 21, Nashua was coupled with Laugh as he was stretched to six furlongs for the first time, in the fifty-second Grand Union Hotel Stakes, worth $15,000-added. Once again, someone else had been flashy enough to catch the bettors' fancy, and the entry was second choice at almost 3-1 in a field of six. C. V. Whitney's Pyrenees had made one of those soul-satis-fying debuts that leave Saratoga fans with a sense of limitless possibilities. Then, a week before the Grand Union, he had run a sterling race in the Saratoga Special, losing by a bare nose to Royal Coinage, with none other than Summer Tan two lengths behind.

From the standpoint of the form players, Pyrenees' being preferred to Nashua followed some logic: Royal Coinage had won the Sapling by nearly a length from Royal Note, the colt who had beaten Nashua; then Pyrenees had lost by only a nose to Royal Coinage, with daylight over Summer Tan, who had been lapped on Nashua in the Juvenile.

Add the long layoff and Nashua had two strikes against him, and conditions stating he give Pyrenees seven pounds (122 to 115) could well be interpreted as strike three. The bettors, of course, perhaps had little way to know that Eddie Arcaro — the premier rider of the day — had established in his mind that Nashua was his choice of two-year-old mounts that year. Also, after the lolling about in the stretch of the Cherry Hill, Fitzsimmons had put blinkers on Nashua for the first time. (It was to be but one in a sequence of blinkers-on, off, on-again with that challenging animal.)

James Cox Brady's third-choice Commonwealth brashly took a three-length lead with a quarter-mile in :23, but Arcaro had Nashua a head in front of him after a half-mile in :46 3/5. In the stretch, Nashua made off to a two-length lead, and although Pyrenees made his run, the odds-on choice could not make much impression. Nashua won by one and three-quarters lengths in 1:12 2/5.

Most of the Saratoga meeting had gone by before Nashua's appearance at the old Spa track, and it was only a week later he went to the post for the climactic juvenile race of the meeting. This was the Hopeful, a $30,000-added race at the time that asked two-year-olds to step up to six and a half furlongs. The 1954 running marked the fiftieth anniversary of the Hopeful, whose forty-nine earlier winners had included Peter Pan, Man o' War, Morvich, Boojum, El Chico, Bimelech, Whirlaway, Pavot, Battlefield, and Native Dancer.

Once again coupled with Laugh (who never seemed to have one), Nashua in his fifth race was favored for the first time. The entry closed at 55-100, barely more than 1-2, although Summer Tan and Pyrenees were back again. All eight runners carried 122 pounds.

Arcaro put Nashua on the lead from the outset, and they would spend the trip turning back one challenge after another. First Commonwealth accompanied him through a half-mile in :46 4/5, and then Eric Guerin, riding Pyrenees that day, took a swing, but Arcaro went to the whip and Nashua turned them back. Then, Bill Boland came rattling up with Summer Tan, but Nashua would let him advance no further than his brawny shoulder and won by a neck.

Not for the first time, Nashua's efforts were described by one Evan Shipman. This was a fellow who put in an appearance in *A Movable Feast* for his amiable drinking days at the Lilas (café) with Ernest Hemingway, in a Paris of shimmery recollection. By 1954, Shipman was lending his own considerable writ-

ing talents to the Turf, specifically *Daily Racing Form*. His reprise of the Hopeful in that publication's *American Racing Manual* is instructive on how this Nashua character was working his way into racing's respect, even without the spectacular margins often required for young stars:

"Repeated challenges, turned back one after the other, even though they were launched by colts of genuine class, are what distinguished this Hopeful from a flock of juvenile stakes that turn out to be 'good' races and nothing more. Purposely, we have reserved mention of the time, feeling that those figures, for all their merit, should be subordinated to the general impression of superlative class gained on this occasion.

"You know now what Nashua did; here is how he did it in terms of the watch. The Saratoga strip...merits the adjectives safe, slow, deep, holding this season, and last Saturday was no exception. Yet Nashua ran his 6 1/2 furlongs (in 1:17 4/5) within four-fifths of a second of the track mark, jointly held by Boojum and Blue Border, two Thoroughbreds who possessed as much pure speed as any within our memory...

"...the reverberating echoes of that race at the Spa

will persist for some time…his two Saratoga starts were so impressive, so unusual, that we are all asking ourselves when we have seen Nashua's like. In all our experience, we never saw a better 2-year-old race than Nashua's Hopeful."

Having created such an impression of potential greatness, Nashua next went out and lost. Not only was he beaten, but he invited questions as to his inherent balance of quality and quirkiness.

Three weeks went by after the Hopeful. Then Nashua came out for the six and a half-furlong Cowdin Stakes, a $25,000-added race at his headquarters, Aqueduct. For all Shipman's superlatives, the crowd was not handing the prize to the Belair colt without reservation. Nashua, under top weight of 124 pounds, was giving up to fourteen pounds to the nine others. He was favored, but at more than even money at 5-4, with Summer Tan, under 120 pounds, the second choice at 3-1.

Four horses battled as a unit in the early going. Nashua was right in there for the tussle, while Guerin, back on Summer Tan, was seventh for the first half-mile. The 30-1 shot Sound Barrier was credited with the rapid fractions — :22 3/5, :45 1/5, 1:09 2/5 — and

a head margin at each call. Arcaro was later quoted as saying he had been told to try taking Nashua back, and he apparently tried to do so a time or two. At any rate, the horse doing the real running down the lane was Summer Tan, who swished through along the rail and not only took command, but drew right out to win by one and a half lengths in 1:16. The time, again, was something for the record books, a new standard for the distance at Aqueduct.

To be beaten by that margin while holding three-quarters of a length over third-placed Bunny's Babe was not a poor performance for Nashua. Still Arcaro's (quoted) exaggeration that Nashua "spit out the bit" as early as the three-eighths pole indicated the colt might have sulked when not allowed to run the way he wished. Clearly, he did not truly give it up at that stage, but he was christened with the Arcaro tattoo through the stretch and was not able, or willing, to close ground once Summer Tan took over.

Ten days later, Nashua was back in action. The New York season had returned to Belmont Park, and he was again on the old Widener Chute, for the six-furlong Anticipation Purse. The "anticipation" was for the

Belmont Futurity, which for many years had owned pride of place among juvenile races. The allowance race had a stakes-quality field, for Nashua faced Royal Coinage, Pyrenees, Washington Park Futurity winner Georgian, and three others, everyone carrying 118 pounds. Nashua was favored, at a nickel over even money.

Nashua broke well, but that time allowed Arcaro to take him back, apparently without ill temper, and was fourth after a half-mile. He then put in a fine run and took over from Royal Coinage, feeling the whip only once to edge out and win by a length. The time once more was extraordinary, 1:08 1/5, equaling the track record down a strip that many a sterling runner had striven.

Fitzsimmons had turned eighty that summer, so it was natural that milestones along the way would be pointed out to him. Nashua's Hopeful had been the old man's first win in the race, and now there was a sentimental side of the racing world thinking how nice it would be if Mr. Fitz were to win the Futurity for the first time. It is perhaps more an indication of the sort of horse, the sort of schedule, and the sort of agenda Mr. Woodward bred and sought that none of the Belair cracks had won the most important juvenile test. On

the other hand, the Futurity had an ambivalent standing. Its winner routinely was regarded as the two-year-old champion and the pro-tem favorite for the next year's Kentucky Derby — especially if he later added any of several available longer, but less rich races. A cloud on that standing was the fact the Futurity had been run since 1888 and for the great majority of those years you could count its winners that also won the Derby on one hand — by joining the tips of the thumb and forefinger. No Futurity winner had added the Derby until Citation in 1947-48. Moreover, with the advent of the one and one-sixteenth-mile Garden State Stakes as the richest race, not only for the division, but the richest in the world, the territory had been altered.

Nonetheless, the reverence for the Futurity, and Mr. Fitz, was such that The Jockey Club chairman, George D. Widener, had secretly arranged for a special, extra, trophy to be produced on Fitzsimmons' behalf — just in case. The sixty-fifth running of the $50,000-added Futurity on October 9 produced a spirited three-horse battle that might have had Mr. Widener thinking "well, there's a wasted bit of silver."

Nashua's superb run in the Anticipation Purse had

again convinced the public he was the one, the Cowdin notwithstanding. Nashua was 3-5, Summer Tan nearly 3-1. Royal Coinage was nearly 5-1, and the four others were long shots. Each of the seven carried 122 pounds.

Hal Price Headley's Georgian set out in front, with Nashua and Summer Tan close together on one rail, while Royal Coinage was farther out toward the middle of the track. The first two fractions were :22 4/5 and :45 1/5, after which Georgian still owned a length lead. The three favorites then swallowed him and entered the final furlongs as a troika, and a vigorous one. Nashua was in the middle, and Arcaro went to the whip once, but then resorted to the sort of "hand ride" that identified the phrase with him more than any other rider of his time.

There were half-inch slits cut in the back of each cup of Nashua's blinkers. If the haughty colt needed more notice of his adversaries' hunger for his downfall than nature provides via instinct and trembling ground, perhaps he could catch a glimpse out the rear-view mirror. Nashua was tested, left and right, but he would not give in. Summer Tan was creeping closer, but Nashua had a head on him at the wire, while the runner-up had eased out to three-quarters of a length over Royal Coinage. The time was good, 1:15 3/5, which was one and one-fifth seconds slower than the straight course world record set sixteen years earlier by Porter's Mite in the Champagne and matched by Native Dancer in 1952.

Guerin's linguistically inventive comment of praise for his mount, Summer Tan, was also a tribute to the victor: "He did everything the winner did, but pass him."

The special trophy had to be delivered in the winner's circle to Mr. Fitz' son John, for the father was at home with a cold. At eighty, one is entitled to admit to this age, even if he is winning a thing called the "futurity."

Nashua earned $88,015, by far his biggest purse of the year, but it was not the intent that his year had ended. The Champagne Stakes and the ultra-rich Garden State Stakes loomed ahead. There was only one week between the Futurity and the Champagne, with an additional two weeks then until the Garden State.

First, an announcement in *The Blood-Horse* dated October 23 stated that William Woodward Jr. said Nashua had a slight cold and would be retired for the year. Later, however, Fitzsimmons was quoted in the same publication that a touch of colic had caused the colt to be withdrawn from "the Jersey race," clearly referring to the Garden State.

Whatever the nuances behind the scenes in the Belair camp were, there was not much subtlety to the Garden State itself. Summer Tan won by nine lengths, collaring the first prize of $151,096.

The official designation of Thoroughbred champions had begun in American racing with polls commenced in 1936. Before then, the status of champion of a division in any given year was subject to the interpretation of whosoever might be writing, or speaking, on the subject. In 1954, there were two major polls, those conducted by *Daily Racing Form* and the Thoroughbred Racing Associations. There was also the Experimental Free Handicap, commenced by Walter Vosburgh in 1933, then inherited by John B. Campbell. The 1954 season marked the first time the Experimental mantle had been handed on to Campbell's successor as the New York racing secretary, F. E. (Jimmy) Kilroe.

The polls both selected Nashua as champion, and so champion he was. But on the Experimental, a mental exercise evaluating two-year-old form complicated by

projecting it to a one and one-sixteenth-mile race the following spring, Kilroe gave pride of place to Summer Tan. The weights were 128 for the Firestone colt, 127 for Nashua, a compliment to both since 126 had long been unofficially established as what would be assigned the "average" topweight of the division.

In giving the Garden State winner the ultimate ranking, Kilroe had a hint of precedent exactly one year old. In 1953, Porterhouse and Hasty Road had each come first in one of the ballotings, but the first Garden State winner, Turn-to, had been co-topweight with Futurity winner Porterhouse on Campbell's Experimental.

Nashua ended the year with six wins in eight races and earnings of $192,865. Wheatley's High Voltage joined him in the Fitzsimmons stable as a champion, being the choice among two-year-old fillies. By the unique and specific rhythms of the racing calendar, the months from November through February would be a "winter" of delicious anticipation.

CHAPTER 3

How It Came To Be

S unny Jim Fitzsimmons and the Belair Stable had
embarked on many a classic campaign in the
past. In the 1930s, the results had been exceedingly
gratifying — ten classic victories. However, there had
been none since Florida racing began occupying the
winters of many top stables, so fifteen years had passed
since Johnstown gave Belair its last quaff from a classic
cup. The 1940s and first years of the 1950s had not
been nearly so luxuriant as the 1930s. There was a fair
share of major winners, including the distaff champion
Vagrancy, but nothing came to fruition in a Triple
Crown race.

Belair Stud had been in operation for some time
before teaming with Fitzsimmons. Woodward later
wrote in a personal history of his stable that his love of
racing was germinated from boyhood days of the 1880s

when his father would take him in a fine carriage out from Manhattan to the races on Long Island. At breakfast one day, his father commented about Pierre Lorillard's being the only American to win the English Derby, creating a specific ambition in the young Woodward's sporting breast. Classic races at historic tracks fueled the young man's interest in the sport, but they were not the origin of Woodward's adventure as a breeder and owner.

After Groton and Harvard, he went to England and became secretary to Joseph Choate, the U.S. ambassador to England. It was a perfect setting to round off young Woodward — the sunset of the Victorian era, the ceremony of government affairs, and enough time to follow the careers of great racehorses.

Woodward returned to the United States in 1903 and went about a business career, rising to chair the Hanover National Bank. Career and family came first, but racing was never out of his thought and ambitions. When so-called reform threatened the very existence of racing in New York and elsewhere, young Woodward conceived of a participation in the sport that would be geared toward "saving" the American Thoroughbred.

The crisis in American racing would come and pass, but Woodward's dreams of the Turf were not diminished.

An uncle owned Belair, a historic mansion in Maryland, and it was there that Woodward had a barn built to quarter the three $100 mares he bought somewhat precipitously. Next came Capt. Hancock, a stallion purchased for $60 after being spotted by Andrew Jackson, a black fellow who worked for Belair. "So, Belair Stud started with an expenditure of $360," Woodward wrote years later — forgetting to add in whatever his uncle insisted he pay for the barn construction.

Capt. Hancock sired the filly Aile d'Or out of one of Woodward's $100 mares. Aile d'Or became the first winner for Woodward in 1909 at the half-mile Marlboro track in Maryland. Woodward named her after a song, "Fantasies, aux Aile d'Or," he had heard in a revue in Paris in 1906.

Even in his days training at the most ramshackle of outlaw tracks, Sunny Jim Fitzsimmons probably never undertook so informal a training regimen as Aile d'Or's. The owner, future chairman of The Jockey Club, took a direct part in this training: "We trained Aile d'Or on the county road, which was sandy at that

time. I would ride a well-bred hunter, and a close friend of mine, P. A. Clark, would ride another, and we would station ourselves about 100 or 200 yards in front of the mare, she ridden by Andrew Jackson (who had once been a jockey for Maryland Governor Oden Bowie)." The Thoroughbred filly and the old black jockey would come rumbling along and overtake them "and this is the way we trained her, and she won. This can be called the first success of Belair Stud."

In time, Aile d'Or foaled Woodward's first stakes winner, the 1920 Toboggan Handicap victor Lion d'Or. In those early days, Woodward raced his horses in Clark's name. Clark was also instrumental in a key moment for the stable in 1914, and, again, it represented rather abrupt decision making. On a rare weekend retreat to his place in Newport, Rhode Island, Woodward noted that Edmond Blanc, a leading French breeder, was selling five daughters of Ajax in an auction in Paris. They appealed to Woodward, but the sale was the next day. Clark, however, was with him and knew the right parties to iron out the logistics forthwith, and soon Belair owned five Ajax mares for a total of $3,750. While these mares were to form a fine nucleus for what came later, it took several years for them to reach the United States from war-torn Europe.

Woodward for most of his career boarded his mares at Claiborne Farm in Kentucky, and he was associated with the Hancock family of Claiborne in standing various stallions. The Woodward weanlings were transferred to Belair, where he could enjoy seeing them in their paddocks whenever he was able to visit the estate, which in due course passed into his ownership.

The French mares arrived with a variety of offspring, and one of them was a yearling filly by Durbar II and out of the mare La Flambee who was named Flambette and won the 1921 Coaching Club American Oaks. ("I was one of the founders of that race, and always liked to have a starter," wrote Woodward of the major filly event launched in 1917.) Flambette eventually became the second dam of Triple Crown winner Omaha and the champion mare Gallorette.

Woodward became thoroughly immersed in the sport and conduct of Thoroughbred racing. He served twenty years as chairman of The Jockey Club, and he cared about his stable to the extent that he wrote a memoir of Gallant Fox's Triple Crown as well as two

separate histories of his English and American stables. In the Gallant Fox book, this closet Turf writer revealed bits of sentiment and color as well as a horseman's strongly held convictions about his horses.

Gallant Fox's most famous defeat came when he and Whichone dueled each other so ruinously in the mud of the 1930 Travers Stakes that a 100-1 shot named Jim Dandy came along to plant his name firmly in history. The defeat rankled Woodward. "The bull-headed (Sonny) Workman (Whichone's rider) merely threw everything to the wind, in his endeavor to beat The Fox at all costs. These are not criticisms or excuses — they merely constitute my analysis of the race," he wrote.

The next paragraph showed another side to his complete involvement: "I went to the stable after the race and was glad to find the horse in very satisfactory shape. I had not been well for a week or ten days and Fitzsimmons asked me how I felt. I told him I was better, and in his usual smiling, friendly way, he told me we could well afford to lose the Travers as long as 'W. W.' felt better."

The Gallant Fox book also gave a remarkable glimpse at a whimsical side of Woodward. This was not detected in the stern face looking out from the pages of the trade publications, or most of his statements made for attribution. After Gallant Fox's retirement, Woodward and his family received a note of congratulations from Rimrock, Arizona, from friends who signed themselves Romaine and (his wife) Virginia. The Woodward response was to compose a poem of seven stanzas, in which it is conjectured how the Westerner Romaine might like to utilize such a horse as Gallant Fox:

"Would you rather ride on him in the great rodeo?/Where broncos buck six feet, he'd buck sixty fo'/ Would you rather rope from him a strong white-faced calf?/ To show how it's done in a second and half—"

The final note appended to the poem was the instruction: "Improve, set to music, and sing."

By the late 1920s, Woodward had begun annually sending one or two yearlings to Cecil Boyd-Rochfort to train in England. He was acting on his boyhood determination to become the second American to win the greatest of all races, the Epsom Derby. The title was still open, technically. Lorillard had won the Derby with an American-bred, Iroquois, in 1881. William Collins Whitney won the

Derby with Volodyovski, who was leased, in 1901, but the winner was not an American-bred.

Woodward never achieved his goal, although he came within a photo finish with Prince Simon in 1950. He did, however, win four classic races in England, as well as the wonderful Ascot Gold Cup, and in general had an exceptional record given the small number he had in training there at any given time.

Ironically, it was the year after Woodward's death in 1953 that the role of second American to win the Derby was filled. It was taken by Robert Sterling Clark, whose Kentucky homebred Never Say Die won the 1954 running. Never Say Die was by Nasrullah, as was Nashua, one of Woodward's projected English candidates among his yearlings of 1953.

Woodward died at the age of seventy-seven on September 26, 1953. The yearlings meant for Boyd-Rochfort had not been sent abroad. Among Woodward's children, one of the four daughters, Edith, had demonstrated the strongest interest and deepest knowledge of the Turf. Woodward's upbringing and approach to life, however, made passing on the stable to his son, William Jr., irresistible. Nor was the young, handsome William Jr. devoid of experience or knowledge about racing. The father had written with obvious pride in the Gallant Fox memoir that when jockey Earl Sande was kicked before a race: "I left the stand quickly to see what had happened. My boy Billy had been with me and when I reached the place I found he was still with me, having made up his mind in a jiffy to stay with it. Sande was carried to the jockey house and his leg was in bad shape, although nothing was broken." Billy was ten years old at the time.

When stewardship of Belair passed to William Jr., he was often described as a son who had not been known for frequenting of the racetrack. However, Humphrey S. Finney, who was called upon to evaluate the Belair horses for estate purposes, wrote years later that he was pleasantly surprised at how much young Junior knew about his father's horses.

(In later years, the sister, Edith Woodward, who married Tom Bancroft Sr., formed a small partnership with her mother, the elegant grande dame Elsie Woodward. They bred and raced the 1967 Horse of the Year, Damascus, and other major winners, reviving the old Belair silks. Mrs. Bancroft apparently wanted to

make a point of establishing her own contacts, for she boarded the mares at John A. Bell III's Jonabell Farm in Kentucky, where Damascus was foaled. The Bancrofts' sons, Thomas Jr. and William, then used the silks for their Pen-Y-Bryn Stable until dissolving it in 1995. They, too, added more distinction to the grand old silks, as their Highland Blade was second in the Belmont Stakes and won the Brooklyn Handicap and Marlboro Cup in the 1980s. The influence of the Bancroft stable still resonates. The Pen-Y-Bryn stakes winner Bailjumper sired Skip Trial, he, in turn, the sire of the 1998 Horse of the Year and $9-million earner Skip Away.)

It is intriguing to contemplate what the results might have been had William Woodward Sr. been given a couple of more years of life. Surely, another Nasrullah colt racing abroad would have been interesting for the English and Irish to have followed. After all, Nasrullah had risen to the top there as a stallion. A Nashua in England likely would have been targeted for Royal Ascot in June, then perhaps the Middle Park Stakes, before being put away to prepare for the classics: the Two Thousand Guineas, Derby, and St. Leger.

He would have faced Our Babu (Guineas winner), Phil Drake (Derby), and the grand filly Meld (St. Leger). No matter how he fared against these, however, hanging over him would have been the greatness of the Italian- and French-raced Ribot. At some point, Nashua might well have faced that unbeaten wonder, perhaps when Ribot ventured to England for the King George VI and Queen Elizabeth Stakes or in one of his two runnings of France's Prix de l'Arc de Triomphe.

But, Woodward Sr. did die, and Woodward Jr. did decide to keep Nashua at home.

The horse apparently had been named prior to the old man's death. The name was easily suggested by the pedigree (Nasrullah—Segula), but that Woodward would think back to his old school and name the colt for a river that ran past Groton might have indicated a sense of special potential. (This cannot be taken as certain. Who knows what goes into naming? Paul Mellon, for example, had turned out many good horses bred at his Rokeby Farms when suddenly he decided to name a horse Rokeby — and it was far from the most fashion-able of horses he had to choose from for that honor!)

Nasrullah was one of the most colorful of horses,

and he turned out to be one of the best of stallions. Years before, William Woodward Sr. had participated in A. B. Hancock Sr.'s importation of the French horse Sir Gallahad III to Claiborne Farm in Kentucky, and the horse had sired Gallant Fox and a host of other important sons and daughters. In the 1940s, Hancock's son, A. B. (Bull) Hancock Jr., was frustrated in his first attempts to buy Nasrullah but was not dissuaded by the obstacles. His eventual acquisition of the horse was one of the most important developments in North American Thoroughbred bloodstock in the second half of the 20th century.

Nasrullah was a son of the unbeaten Nearco and out of Mumtaz Begum, she, in turn, a daughter of the great race filly Mumtaz Mahal.

This family was a fertile ground for stallion production. In addition to Nasrullah, Mumtaz Begum also foaled the dam of another influential import, the stallion Royal Charger. Moreover, the next dam, Mumtaz Mahal, was also the dam of Mah Mahal, she, in turn, the dam of the leading sire Mahmoud, also imported to Kentucky.

Nasrullah was bred by the Aga Khan (grandfather of the

present Aga Khan). Just as Nashua was to be, Nasrullah was seen as a handsome, powerful colt of unlimited potential but erratic personality. Even the son perhaps was never quite so frustrating as Nasrullah himself.

Nasrullah won the Coventry Stakes and another race and finished second in the Middle Park Stakes from a total of four starts at two in England. He was ranked best among colts and one pound below the Nearco filly Lady Sybil on the Free Handicap for 1942. V. R. Orchard, writing in *The Bloodstock Breeders' Review*, stated that "his high place in the Free Handicap is hardly justified by his running." Orchard softened, however, in addressing the physical properties of the colt: "Whatever else may be said of Nasrullah, it is clear that he is a colt of character. In appearance he is a rich bay of commanding proportions. His quarters are immensely powerful, and any good judge of a horse would put down this fine-looking colt as near perfect as possible if considering him apart from his racecourse performance."

At three, Nasrullah won his seasonal debut, in the one-mile Chatteris Stakes, but only after slowing suddenly while in the lead. (A similar description could be

used for Nashua's debut at three.) He was fourth in the
Two Thousand Guineas and third in the Epsom Derby. It
was the ability to place in the one and a half-mile Derby
added to his success at two that made Bull Hancock
covet the horse as an American stallion prospect.

Nashua's sire relented to win the Cavensham Stakes
to the relief of trainer Frank Butters, but in the St.
Leger he never made the lead and finished sixth as the
fillies Herringbone and Ribbon ran one-two. In the one
and a quarter-mile Champion Stakes, over a straight
course at Newmarket, the great jockey Sir Gordon
Richards more or less tricked Nasrullah into winning.
He waited with such patience that by the time
Nasrullah got to the lead, it was all right if he then
sulked, for they had just sailed past the finish line. (Ted
Atkinson would use a similar tactic on Nashua in the
Wood Memorial.)

Phil Bull of the English publication *Timeform* commented in *Racehorses of 1943*: "Last year, I regarded
Nasrullah as head and shoulders above the other colts of
his age. I gave him a long and rather enthusiastic write
up, and, in spite of his having failed in each of his classic ventures, in spite of his bad temper, his mulish antics,

in spite of his exasperating unwillingness to do the job, etc., I fear that I am going to give him another write up. I know he doesn't deserve it, but I can't help it."

Either Bull or a staff member underscored that ambivalence with captions under photos, such as "Nasrullah pretending to be a gentleman"; "Nasrullah condescends to pass the post in front in the Chatteris Stakes"; "Nasrullah impersonating a mule."

The colt had a two-year career of five wins from ten starts and earnings of $15,240 during a time of wartime purses.

Hancock tried to buy him, offering $50,000, but was too late. Nasrullah was sent to stud at Barton Stud, Suffolk, England, before being sent to Ireland. He had been plucked by prominent Irish breeder Joe McGrath. Hancock chased Nasrullah for several years. At one point, a deal seemed to be struck, with Woodward, Harry Guggenheim, and E. P. Taylor joining Hancock. Taylor was doing the deal, in pounds, but the £100,000 price was befuddled by imminent devaluation of the English currency.

A year later, in 1950, Nasrullah was ten and a proven success abroad, while one of his sons, Noor, had been

imported and would rack up four wins over the great Citation. Hancock described his ultimate success as coming after "a lot of negotiation." This included a meeting with seller Joe McGrath and lawyers in New York City and a British bank holiday which fell near or on the agreed deadline. This meant the "earnest money" did not get recorded by the necessary date, although from Hancock's perspective he had sent it "in time."

Hancock and McGrath hit it off as horsemen and worked out the deal. Nasrullah finally arrived at Claiborne in the summer of 1950. By the end of 1951, his status had been elevated, as he led the sire list in England. His first American foal crop was born in 1952, and Nashua was included.

Nasrullah quickly became the first stallion to lead both the English and American sire lists. He lived to nineteen, dying in 1959, and he eventually led the American list five times: 1955, 1956, 1959, 1960, and 1962. Only Star Shoot, Bull Lea, and Bold Ruler matched that achievement during the 20th century; Bold Ruler, who led the list a total of eight times, was a son of Nasrullah.

Also among the most significant of Nasrullah's ninety-eight stakes winners (twenty-three percent) were the aforementioned English Derby-St. Leger winner Never Say Die, plus Never Bend, Bald Eagle, Jaipur, Leallah, Delta, Nadir, Bug Brush, Grey Sovereign, and Nasrina. Nasrullah sired nine voted champions in North America.

Never Bend sired Mill Reef, head of a flourishing branch of the sire line in Europe, while in this country the Nasrullah sire line lately has been buttressed by Blushing Groom, Caro, Seattle Slew, A.P. Indy, and others.

The female family that produced Nashua traced to France. Woodward had bought the early draft of mares there, and Sir Gallahad III also came from France, so it was a country of ongoing importance to the Belair Stud. In 1930, Woodward imported a filly by Sardanapale—Prosopopee, by Sans Souci. She was a yearling and had been bred by Maurice de Rothschild. Her sire, Sardanapale, had won the French Derby and Grand Prix de Paris in 1914 and led the French sire lists of 1922 and 1927. He was an influence for classic-distance stamina as a sire and broodmare sire. Sardanapale's offspring included the Grand Prix de Paris and Prix Royal Oak winner Fiterari, as well as

Apelle and Doniazade. Produce of Sardanapale's daughters eventually included the two-time Prix de l'Arc de Triomphe winner Corrida.

Woodward's Sardanapale filly was named Sekhmet. She was unraced at two in 1931, then failed to place as a three-year-old, but she was kept for the stud. Her first seven foals were fillies, and while that might be seen as a fine thing for developing a broodmare band, the negative aspect was that they were failing to distinguish themselves for the most part. Her 1938 filly, Booklet, by Sir Gallahad III, was one sent abroad, but was sold to Lady Zia Werhner before being stakes-placed. (Booklet foaled five stakes winners.)

In 1942, Sekhmet foaled Segula, to the cover of Johnstown. A racehorse of exceptional quality, Johnstown had won the Derby and Belmont of 1939, but was to prove very moderate as a sire of runners, getting only six stakes winners (three percent). Sekhmet eventually foaled nine fillies from twelve foals, and Booklet and Segula were the only ones to place in stakes.

The campaign that Fitzsimmons prescribed for Segula was very much within the heavy racing philosophy. She did not race at two, but then made twenty-nine starts at three and twenty at four. She won in her second start, and in her fourth was tried in stakes company for the first time, making no impression in Gallorette's Acorn Stakes. As Woodward said, he liked to have a runner in the Coaching Club American Oaks, and Segula was his representative in 1945. She finished third, which looks nice on her record, but it was not a particularly distinguished performance. She merely raced along well enough to finish in the middle of a five-filly field as Elpis won from Monsoon. The Belair filly was beaten by eight and a half lengths. Still, to be effective at all at one and three-eighths miles, along with her later front-running victories in sprints, gave Segula at least some qualifications as a race mare with a bit of class.

She wound up winning six of her twenty-nine races at three, but was last in Ace Card's Gazelle in her only later stakes attempt that year. At four, Segula placed in one additional stakes, the Hannah Dustin, also won by Elpis. Her best placement seemed to be in what were called class D handicaps, of which she won several. She did go out on a good note, for in her last race, a one and one-sixteenth-mile event of that category, she led throughout to score at the Empire City meeting at Jamaica. The fractions were :23 4/5, :47 3/5, 1:13 3/5, 1:39, with a final time of 1:46.

Segula thus owned a record of nine wins in forty-nine starts and earned $35,015. Joseph A. Estes later wrote of her that, "Though she was not a stakes winner herself, Segula was a better racer than most of the mares which qualify as such." It is difficult to see just what merited such praise, unless he were giving particularly high marks for rugged soundness.

From the pattern of her mates, it is not easy to determine just where Segula ranked in prestige within the Belair broodmare band. None of her first three foals was by any of the top echelon of Claiborne's stallions. Her first two were by Some Chance, winner of the Futurity, Gallant Fox Handicap, and a fine run of other stakes. Segula's next foal was by Alsab, a champion racehorse, but off-bred; although eventually to prove only moderate at stud, the youngish Alsab was represented by the 1948 champion juvenile filly, Myrtle Charm, the year before Segula went to Alsab.

The Alsab—Segula filly, named Sabette and foaled

in 1950, was to turn around the lack of stakes success
for the family. However, the decision to include Segula
in the first American book of the classy Nasrullah was
made when Sabette was but a yearling. Whether it was
an indication of disenchantment with the family or
not, Fitzsimmons and Woodward risked Sabette once
for a $7,500 claiming price in September of her two-
year-old year, 1952. Fortunately for them, she was not
taken. At three, Sabette progressed into a high-class
filly. In the much-coveted CCA Oaks, she and jockey
Higley closed four lengths in the final furlong and
failed by only a nose to overtake the eventual champion, Grecian Queen. Later, in Saratoga's historic
Alabama Stakes at one and a quarter miles, jockey
Higley kept the star billing for once, and he brought
her along in time to defeat Grecian Queen while getting twelve pounds. Sabette also had a win over nice
older fillies and mares, in the Diana Handicap. This was
in 1953, the year Woodward Sr. died, and a month
afterward, Sabette added the Gallorette Stakes on
behalf of William Jr.

Sabette won seven of thirty-one races and earned
$80,755. That record was certainly sufficient to vital-

ize the female family and focus considerable attention on her handsome younger half-brother. Nashua, Segula's Nasrullah colt, had been foaled at Claiborne on April 14, 1952.

The admiring Evan Shipman, having followed Nashua's progress at two, announced his satisfaction of how Fitzsimmons turned out the colt when he reappeared at three: Nashua "had been a big, growthy 2-year-old. He was built on rugged lines, and he might have been described at that age as a bit coarse, although there was nothing about his conformation or individuality that did not delight a practical horseman. He kept on growing during his let-up, and, as is often the case, as he matured, his lines achieved refinement and definition. Nashua always had character, but he was also a beautiful colt when he came out to make his seasonal debut as a 3-year-old, and that is an adjective that would hardly have been applied the previous season."

As the old trainer and the new owner addressed the 1955 season, Nashua was ready.

A View To Thrill

G iving a colt a break between his juvenile season and the launch of his classic campaign may be spoken of as giving the youngster "plenty of time." This approach doesn't leave much margin for error, though, once the let-up phase is completed and serious work has begun anew. With Nashua, Fitzsimmons stressed long foundation-building gallops, with the fifty-nine-year-old exercise rider, Bill McCleary, aboard. This meant the big colt was building his muscles under a weight of about 145 pounds. Jockey Ted Atkinson would be brought in on occasion when a breeze was on the colt's docket.

The first target in terms of a race was a seven-furlong allowance event on February 9. This would make his comeback exactly four months after he last raced, in the Belmont Futurity. A heavy South Florida rain had drenched the track, however, and on the appointed day it was drying out, likely a bit lumpy, and Fitzsimmons declined. Instead, he put Atkinson up two days later for a serious move, and Nashua dashed off six furlongs in 1:10 2/5. The track record was only one second faster, and on that particular day, the swiftest six-furlong race on the card required 1:11 3/5.

The winter's first major event, the one and one-eighth-mile Flamingo Stakes, was by then only fifteen days away. It was not until February 21, the Monday of Flamingo Week, that Fitzsimmons managed to get another race into Nashua. A betless exhibition was staged at one and one-sixteenth miles, and Eddie Arcaro flew in from California for Nashua's debut. It was a quarter mile farther than Nashua had ever run and involved going around two turns for the first time. Writing about Nashua some years later, Hall of Fame rider Atkinson recalled, "One morning when I worked Nashua, he gave me an indication that he probably could take off like a bird leaving a limb, although I don't think he had ever been asked for real speed from the start in any of his races."

Although there was no betting, this Spanish Moss

Purse was a true race, with a purse of $7,500. Under the allowance conditions, Nashua took up 126 pounds for the first time, giving from nine to twelve to his three rivals. He tried to go wide on the first turn, but Arcaro wrestled him back toward the proper path, and he lay just off the front-running Munchausen. Nashua assumed control, or at least the lead, in the upper stretch. If Arcaro was pleased with the physical development of the colt over the winter, he was about to be disgusted by his behavior. Nashua loafed enough that Arcaro felt the need to give him a good pop with the whip, and he opened up again. Then, a few strides before the finish, Nashua shied from something he noticed, crossed to the rail, and then tried to prop.

The time was adequate, 1:44 1/5. "There's just no way of making him win impressively," Arcaro said, while Fitz quipped that the colt was "counting the house." (Phil Bull might have muttered something that almost rhymed with foolish, i.e., "mulish.")

The press, aided no doubt by the masterful Hialeah publicity man Everett Clay, picked up on Nashua's shenanigans. Each of the next three races seemed to bring out another element of what might have come

off as a charming playfulness to the public, but which Arcaro associated with escalation of gray hair.

Fitzsimmons had put blinkers on Nashua after his third race, and the youngster had worn them for his last six starts. So ineffective was the equipment in helping the horse focus on the work at hand in the Spanish Moss that he took them off for the Flamingo. Nashua was raced barefaced every time out until well into the next year's summer.

Nashua faced eleven horses in the Flamingo Stakes, a $100,000-added race having its twenty-sixth running. He was 7-10, with Everglades Stakes winner Prince Noor second choice at 4-1, and Saratoga the third choice at slightly more than 5-1. Atkinson was aboard Saratoga, a sleek and competent Blenheim II colt raced by Marion du Pont Scott.

Apollo opened a lead of three lengths early, with Nashua settling into second. The longshot on the lead was fading after a half-mile, and Nashua edged in front. Saratoga hooked him, and they battled together into the stretch. Nashua came out, and the two seemed to brush before Arcaro whipped and drove the favorite out to win by one and a half lengths. The time for the nine furlongs on a fast track was 1:49 3/5, which was some two seconds over the track record. Atkinson claimed foul, but the finish order was allowed to stand. Arcaro noted that Nashua "ran a little more kindly, but he was still fooling around. If he had run as he should, he would have won by ten."

Gulfstream Park's $100,000-added Florida Derby, in its fourth modern running, had gained status nearly equal the Flamingo's, and this one and one-eighth-mile event was the later of the two major classic preps in the South Florida season. It was run on March 26, exactly a month after the Flamingo. Fitzsimmons had returned to New York with the rest of the stable, but Nashua stayed in Florida with assistant Bart Sweeney.

Public confidence was not enhanced, at least insofar as the mutuel pool expresses such things. Nashua was not as strong a favorite as he had been in the Flamingo, going off at nearly even money (95-100), with Saratoga slightly over 3-1 as second choice. The Florida Derby was then an allowance race, the top pair being among the highweights at 122 pounds each and the weights dropping down as far as 109 among the seven others.

Saratoga could not handle the deep slop that resulted from a torrential rain and finished last, struggling throughout. Nashua, catching a sloppy track for the first time, was eased back from post position number one, and for only the second time since his debut was behind more than one horse at the first fractional call. First Cabin set sail on the lead, as Arcaro tugged Nashua back to fifth, trying to keep clear on the outside, where he stayed for a half mile. The big horse then moved to second and made his challenge in the upper stretch. First Cabin, in receipt of nine pounds and brave on the lead, fought on for a way farther, but Nashua forged to the front. So far so good, but the tricks were about to start again.

Nashua propped at about the sixteenth pole, and a 21-1 shot named Blue Lem had momentum as he continued his rally from last in the first half-mile. Blue Lem, also getting nine pounds, had been an inglorious 157-1 for the Flamingo, in which he was fourth, but suddenly the greatest jockey of the era was flogging the champion of the division just to get home in front of him. Bathed in the chocolately goo of the soaked track, Nashua relented to do what was necessary to preserve the lead, winning by a neck. Blue Lem had more than two lengths over the game First Cabin. The time was 1:53 1/5, which on that sort of track was indicative of nothing other than the sort of track it was.

Back in New York with Fitzsimmons, Nashua had almost exactly another month before his next race, the Wood Memorial. This was the last pre-classic prep for Gallant Fox in 1930, and it still was the last big test for classic aspirants in New York. It occasioned the renewal of the spirited Nashua-Summer Tan rivalry of their juvenile days.

Summer Tan had had an eventful time since winning the Garden State Stakes. He developed a blood clot soon after and very nearly died. Although he, too, spent part of the winter in Florida, thoughts of the sort of progressive schedule Nashua had been given were erased. Trainer Sherrill Ward did not get Summer Tan back to the races until they returned to New York. He got a one and one-sixteenth-mile race into his recovering star. So sensational was Summer Tan in winning by fifteen lengths that his performance, along with the memory of his facile Garden State score, helped send the less-seasoned colt off as the Wood favorite.

The great sportswriter Red Smith observed of the

coming clash in the Wood Memorial that, "Looking back, one couldn't recall another New York race that created so much advance interest since 1938, when popular imagination was stirred by Belmont's abortive plan to match Seabiscuit and War Admiral (that plan fell through and the pair met later at Pimlico)."

Arcaro had been suspended and was spared the agony and denied the ecstasy of riding Nashua in the Wood Memorial. Atkinson drew the high-pressure assignment. As an aside, it might be noted that, as recalled by Nashua's old friend Clem Florio, "all the Italians and Jews (on the backstretch) liked Arcaro, and the Irish liked Atkinson. It was an ethnic thing, but after awhile it occurred to me, 'Atkinson's the guy out there every day, trying his best, in the mud, whatever, giving you everything; now, Arcaro certainly was not under-motivated, but he was more like 'If I can do this, I'm going to; if I can't, I won't.' "

Atkinson would more likely have applied Florio's second description not to Arcaro, but to Nashua. Atkinson won major races in driving finishes the only two times he rode Nashua in competition, but he was frank in his lack of love for the big galoot. Arcaro's book *I Ride to Win!* came out several years too soon to include Nashua, but in 1961, Atkinson published *All the Way!* (with Lucy Freeman, Paxton-Slade, Inc., New York). In a chapter on Nashua, he observed:

"I knew the type of horse Nashua was emotionally. He was difficult to ride because of his whims, and his rider could be kept in a state of anxious suspense most of the time. I thought if I could handle him right (in the Wood Memorial), I could get a lot out of him, even though he was a horse I didn't particularly like, personally.

"He had a touch of selfishness about him. At times, he wouldn't deliver when asked. The few times he was beaten, and a couple of them rather badly, he seemed to have no excuse but his own obstinacy. However, he did his best in this Wood Memorial, though midway of the race he seemed completely unwilling."

Atkinson at the time was only two years removed from the career of Tom Fool, perhaps as professional, willing — and reliable — as any horse, and with whom he had authored a perfect ten-for-ten season in the handicaps as 1953 Horse of the Year. After that experience, Atkinson did not suffer clowns gladly.

Nashua's personality was sometimes misread as having an element of meanness. Later that year, Fitzsimmons remarked, "I can't get through my head where anybody got the idea he was roguish or ugly. All he wants to do is play. He's always rubber-necking around, and is real smart about what he sees."

The magazine *Sports Illustrated*, then in its second calendar year, certainly considered the Wood Memorial a major event. Arcaro at times would be almost as critical of Nashua as Atkinson was, but the week after the Wood, *Sports Illustrated* ran an article entitled, in Arcaro's words: "Nashua — That Horse I Ride...Wow!"

The Wood Memorial, a one and one-eighth-mile test worth $100,000-added at the old Jamaica racetrack, was run on April 23 and drew five runners. They each carried Triple Crown weight of 126 pounds. Summer Tan, however little racing he had had since the autumn, was heavily favored, bet down almost to 3-5. Nashua was second choice at 6-5. On the Monday of the race, both had worked between races, and Summer Tan had gotten his mile more than a second faster than Nashua's.

Summer Tan's trainer, Sherrill Ward, fretted to

Sports Illustrated: "I don't mind admitting that his 1:37 workout was too fast. Nashua's workout was a good one, too, and maybe some people are forgetting that my horse is a free and willing worker, whereas Nashua's best traits come out in a race. He's (Nashua) a rugged competitor. If he's in front it's a lot easier to get within a length of him than it is to get a length ahead of him. And if he's behind, you know perfectly well he's going to try mighty hard to get you."

In most races run the way the Wood was run, a dispassionate observer might presume "the horse that set the pace had left his race on the track in the work," or conversely, "was short coming off only one start since his illness." Indeed, it could be simplified to: Summer Tan, coming off one race since he looked death in the door, led from the start, seemed to have the race under control, but was passed in the final yards, and the last furlong took fourteen seconds.

As is usually the case in a horse race, however, there were subtleties to interpret.

One of the longshots was a horse named Simmy. Since Atkinson had ridden him when he equaled a world record for six and a half furlongs, he thought

Simmy might help by being the one to press Summer Tan, who was presumed to be the front runner. Summer Tan and Eric Guerin broke with Nashua and Atkinson and soon opened a lead, but since Simmy seemed to get a message from the equine pecking order/class standpoint, it soon was obvious that Atkinson would have no help in keeping Summer Tan honest. The cat-and-mouse game was set up early, and for a time Nashua seemed like he was not playing. Atkinson was known as "the slasher" for his whip action, not because it was overly punishing — although certainly strong enough to be effective — but because of the unique high and round stroke of his whipping motion. He had to get into Nashua early to get him into the game. Nashua then seemed about to draw up to Summer Tan nearing the turn for home, where the front runner drifted out. Nashua seemed disconcerted, and so, at a critical moment, Atkinson again had to wonder what was in the mind of, as he called him, "the big Don Alonso."

Nevertheless, Atkinson wrote later in his book, he had a feeling Nashua had the other horse measured. Summer Tan appeared to be in an all-out drive, and

Ted was still figuring out when would be the best time to give Nashua the prod. He decided to wait, wait, wait until the sixteenth pole. There he brought the whip down "about as hard as I knew how and hollered my fool head off," and just as Nashua had seemed beaten, he surged forward. Atkinson thought he could win by a length, but he misjudged how much Summer Tan had left. Flailing away in the final yards, Atkinson drove his mount to the front. Although Nashua won by a neck, it had seemed that he was behind ten yards from the wire. A blink past the finish, he was clearly in front.

"After the race, everyone who saw it swore up and down they thought I had no chance of catching Summer Tan with less than an eighth of a mile to go," Atkinson wrote. "But I had no doubts...I felt Nashua could win. Very seldom in my career did I have this conviction about a horse until the red board was posted!...Mostly, I remember my strong feeling that coming into the stretch, we had it made."

For the record, Simmy was third, twenty-five lengths behind Summer Tan. The time was 1:50 3/5, just over a second off the track record and equal to the clocking of Native Dancer in the 1953 Wood Memorial.

In a *Sports Illustrated* commentary over Arcaro's byline, the jockey was so warm and cuddly in his remarks after the Wood Memorial that it is impossible to ignore the possibility that he was not altogether sure of getting the mount back. Quoth the rider known as The Master: "...although I've been accused of making a few unkind remarks about Nashua's temperament and running behavior, most of those comments were taken seriously when they should have been taken in jest. Actually, Nashua shows many signs of true greatness. The fact that he has a personality of his own — that he turns on his speed burst when he wants to and not a moment before he wants to — contributes, I think, to his greatness. Last year, I looked on him as a boy with a few playful pranks. This year, I think of him as a man who still likes at times to play like a kid. Be that as it may, he's all man when there's a job to be done."

Nonetheless, in that same article, Arcaro noted that a rider had to "ride him as he finds him" on any given day. One could not be certain from one race to the next what the attitude would be. "He'll unnerve you, he'll thrill you, and he'll worry you," Arcaro commented.

Now, the Kentucky Derby lay immediately ahead.

There had been no Triple Crown winner since Citation in 1948, this lull following four winners within the decade of the 1940s. What no one could know, of course, was that the drought was barely underway. By the time Secretariat won the Triple in 1973, the mystique had grown to near hysterical proportions. But in 1955, the Triple Crown did not loom as the largest of prizes in everyone's eyes. The previous year, for instance, Derby winner Determine was returned to California without even having a go at the Preakness.

Having managed to defeat his old rival Summer Tan in the Wood Memorial, Nashua was faced not only by another challenge from that worthy foe, but a new challenger in the form of Swaps.

Swaps had excited Californians with his Santa Anita Derby victory, and he mightily impressed Kentuckians with his facile sprint victory in a tune-up over the Churchill Downs strip a week before the Derby.

Much was made of the contrasts between the two stables involved. Rex Ellsworth, breeder-owner of the California-bred Swaps, and his trainer and lifelong friend, Meshach (Mesh) Tenney, were Mormon cowboys who eschewed virtually all practices in horsemanship that might be called fancy. They were true and talented horsemen, but on the major racetracks were dealing in a milieu where the word "cowboy" did not always imply a compliment. Tenney slept in the stall with Swaps in the nights before the race, which created a great story line. Fitzsimmons, on the other hand, did not even sleep in the same city or state as Nashua. Nearing age eighty-one, he decided against making the trip to Kentucky and facing the ardor of Derby Week preparation.

Sports Illustrated again was Nashua's foil. The magazine sent no less a literary figure than William Faulkner to sniff and savor Kentucky in springtime — Derby time. Part of Faulkner's essay pulsed of what it was like to watch the Derby favorite during a workout in the week of the holy grail itself. He never used the name Nashua — didn't need to — as he described "the big horse...not even walking. He is strolling. Because he is looking around. Not at us. He has seen people; the sycophant adulant human roar had faded behind his drumming feet too many times for us to hold his attention..."And as the exercise unfolded, Nashua came past, "...a drive and power; something a little raw-boned, not graceless so much as too busy to bother with grace…appearing to skim along just above the top rail like the big diminishing hawk, inflexible and unde-viable, voracious not for meat but for speed and dis-tance." Well, you get Faulkner and you get the goods.

Derby Week invariably conjures many questions about the contenders, including their fondness or lack thereof of the Louisville track's surface. Summer Tan, perhaps wrung out by being rushed to the Wood Memorial and then subjected to such a testing effort, was the one who slipped in public estimation. While some might have written about Swaps as if he were a little-respected outsider from the West, he, in fact, was taken very seriously.

The veteran racing writer Russ Harris has memories of groom Alfred Robertson's observation that, stabled close by Summer Tan, he and others on the Fitzsimmons staff observed a difference in Summer Tan's demeanor and concluded he was no longer the key horse to beat. Fitzsimmons' son John is tabbed in this scenario as failing to read the situation; of course, this was very much an after-the-fact recitation.

At any rate, after the betting had opened at Churchill Downs, and the hour of the one and a quarter-mile Run for the Roses approached, Swaps was the pari-mutuel favorite for some time. Eventually, at post time, Nashua was 6-5 and the Californian second choice at just under 3-1. Summer Tan was off at nearly 5-1 in a smallish Derby field of ten.

Bill Shoemaker had ridden Swaps several times earlier, although John Longden had been aboard for the Santa Anita Derby. Shoe was back aboard for the prep a week before the Derby, and for the big race itself. An earlier rider was John Burton, a young Mormon who was true to his religion, and when it was decided it was time for him to travel on his missionary work, travel he did.

In two books Shoemaker co-authored, he wrote virtually the same memory of the pre-Derby scene. Tenney said, "The reason you're on Swaps today is that Mr. Ellsworth and I think you are a good rider. Now prove it. I want you to lay second or third, but if you can't, use your own judgment. Go get 'em." (*Shoemaker*, by Shoemaker and Barney Nagler, Eclipse Thoroughbred Library, New York, 1988, and, virtually verbatim, *The Shoe*, by Shoemaker and Dan Smith, Rand McNally & Co., 1976.)

Already a three-time leading national rider in both wins and earnings, Shoemaker undoubtedly took heart in knowing that these guys thought he was a good rider. He would try to do his best to "prove it," of course. In an atmospheric afternoon of darkness, rain, and then washing sunlight, the ten aligned, 126 pounds on each, no waiting left — the Run for the Roses, $125,000-added. Nashua was drawn in the middle, post five, Swaps was eight, and Summer Tan ten. Nashua broke on top, but longshot Trim Destiny and Swaps quickly moved to the lead. Swaps assumed command with a quarter-mile in :23 3/5. As Shoemaker later wrote, he had a hold on Swaps, but everyone else seemed to be taking hold, too. He dared hope for the best, and after a half-mile in :47 2/5, he had a length lead over Trim Destiny with Nashua more than three lengths behind him. Shoemaker recalled musing to himself: "Well, if they just let me go a little further like this, they'll never catch me."

An oft-repeated story line afterward was that Sunny Jim's strategy from afar was that Arcaro was to pay a great deal of attention to Summer Tan. Eric Guerin had Summer Tan a length off Nashua after a half-mile.

Nashua, loved by racing fans for his charismatic personality, reached stardom both on the track and on the relatively new medium of television.

Nasrullah (top), Nashua's sire, became the first stallion to lead both the English and American sire lists, ably carrying on the line of his unbeaten sire, Nearco (above left).

Nashua's dam, Segula (left), was a stakes-placed daughter of 1939 Kentucky Derby winner Johnstown (below).

William Woodward Sr. (below) passed on his famed Belair Stud (bottom), which produced the Triple Crown winners Gallant Fox and Omaha, to his ill-fated son, William Woodward Jr. (right, with Nashua and Eddie Arcaro). In late 1955, Woodward Jr. was killed by his wife in what was ruled an accidental shooting.

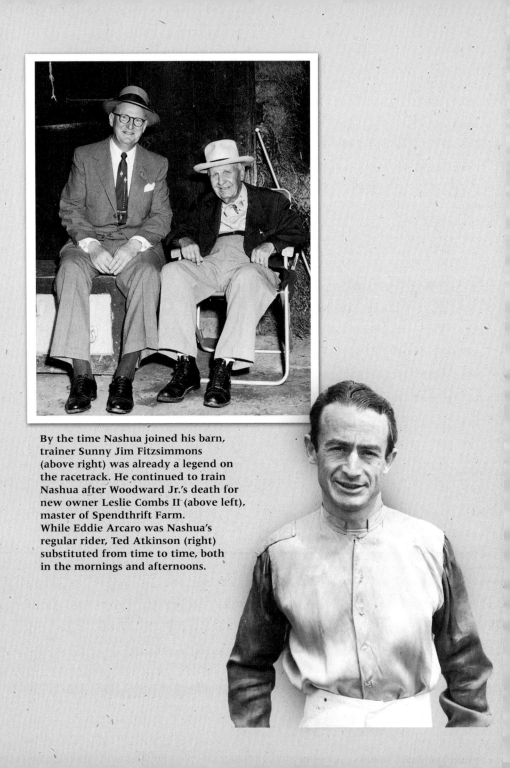

By the time Nashua joined his barn,
trainer **Sunny Jim Fitzsimmons**
(above right) was already a legend on
the racetrack. He continued to train
Nashua after Woodward Jr.'s death for
new owner **Leslie Combs II** (above left),
master of Spendthrift Farm.
While Eddie Arcaro was Nashua's
regular rider, **Ted Atkinson** (right)
substituted from time to time, both
in the mornings and afternoons.

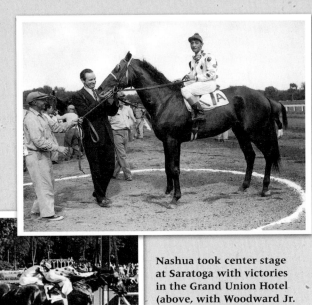

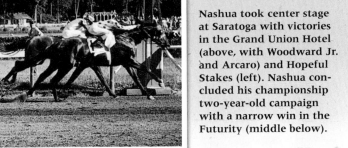

Nashua took center stage at Saratoga with victories in the Grand Union Hotel (above, with Woodward Jr. and Arcaro) and Hopeful Stakes (left). Nashua concluded his championship two-year-old campaign with a narrow win in the Futurity (middle below).

In the spring of 1955, Nashua was impressive on the Triple Crown trail,
with victories in the Flamingo, Florida Derby (below),
and Wood Memorial (above).

A chestnut blur from California named Swaps upended Nashua's Kentucky Derby hopes (right, Swaps in lead), but afterward the West Coast runner went home, leaving the Preakness (below) and Belmont (above) all to Nashua.

Nashua met Swaps again in their famed Match Race at Washington Park on August 31, 1955, and this time Nashua easily prevailed. The connections of both horses were included in the trophy presentation (left). Nashua breezed to victory in the Jockey Club Gold Cup (top) and was named Horse of the Year.

Running in Spendthrift's colors at four, Nashua began the season with a Widener victory (bottom, second from left), coming into the race off works alone. Through an up-and-down year, Nashua posted wins in the Grey Lag (left, middle), Camden, Suburban (below), and Monmouth Handicaps.

Nashua ended his four-year-old season with a repeat victory
in the Jockey Club Gold Cup (below). He left the racetrack
under the watchful eye of Fitzsimmons and in the care
of longtime groom Al Robertson (above) to head
to Kentucky for stud duty.

Nashua presented an imposing figure as he surveyed Belmont Park for the last time (below). Before arriving at Spendthrift Farm, Nashua received a farewell party at Keeneland in Lexington (bottom). Combs, Arcaro, and Fitzsimmons (right) were part of the festivities.

Among Nashua's top offspring were Noble Nashua (top), who fittingly won the Swaps Stakes; Diplomat Way (below), who captured the Blue Grass Stakes; and Shuvee (right), a two-time champion who, like her sire, won the Jockey Club Gold Cup twice.

Nashua left his greatest legacy as a broodmare sire. His stakes-winning daughter Gold Digger (above right) produced the immortal Mr. Prospector (above). Another Nashua mare, Bramalea (below right), is the dam of top racehorse and sire Roberto (below).

The author on a visit to see Nashua in 1959 (right). Nashua became a popular Bluegrass tourist attraction in his years at historic Spendthrift Farm.

SPENDTHRIFT FARM

Nashua remained at Spendthrift until his death in 1982 at the age of thirty. A statue of Nashua and his longtime groom Clem Brooks, sculpted by Liza Todd, graces the central yard of Spendthrift's stallion barn, the "Nashua Motel."

NASHUA
BAY HORSE, NASRULLAH–SEGULA
1952 — 1982

HORSE OF THE YEAR
CHAMPION AT 2 AND 3
WINNER OF 22 RACES $1,288,565
INCLUDING THE PREAKNESS AND BELMONT STAKES
WORLD'S FORMER LEADING MONEY WINNER
SIRE OF 77 STAKES WINNERS
AND THE EARNERS OF MORE THAN $17,000,000

They continued apace, with no real change in position for the next quarter-mile, and Swaps still had his length lead in 1:12 2/5. Shoemaker had gotten his dream ride. Trim Destiny finally began to fall back, but Summer Tan was not making any headway, as Arcaro set sail for the lead. Turning for home, Nashua leveled for his run. There would be no tricks today. He closed almost to even terms. The favorite, "the big horse, was voracious for speed and distance" now. But wait; Shoemaker and Swaps had finessed a mile in 1:37 and still were right there. Shoe later said that Nashua's getting so close was largely because Swaps balked a moment when he spotted the starting gate, still parked near the quarter-mile pole.

In the upper stretch, Nashua ceased to gain. Swaps not only held him off, but turned him back. Swaps edged out to a length lead, then one and a half lengths, and he hit the wire the winner by that margin. The final time was 2:01 4/5, only two-fifths of a second away from Whirlaway's venerated Derby mark from 1941. "Swoosh went Swaps" was Arcaro's comment. Nashua had more than six lengths on Summer Tan, who came home wearily and did not run again that year.

Fitzsimmons immediately assumed the blame, stating that it was his fault that Arcaro had paid too much attention to Summer Tan; by the time Arcaro realized his old foe did not have what it took, it was too late to deal effectively with Swaps. In public comments after the fact, Arcaro complied. However, the crack *Sports Illustrated* racing reporter Whitney Tower had elicited from Arcaro a telling comment before the race: "I don't think we'll have as much trouble from Summer Tan as from Swaps. He's the horse to beat."

Whatever the contradictions of rider's intuition and trainer's instructions might have been, it seems difficult to take at face value that a champion jockey who was twenty-one years past his first Derby ride was fooled. This would mean that Arcaro was psyched out by the presumed prowess of a colt he could clock right off his flank with a glance or two backward, as well as by a front runner on an easy lead after he had already identified that horse as the major threat! On the other hand, if preoccupation with Summer Tan were not the reason Arcaro let Shoe float along so easily, what other reason could there have been?

Tower quoted William Woodward's and Arcaro's

verbal exchange as follows:

"We had no excuse, Eddie. I think he was beaten by a better horse today."

"Yep. Swaps was better — today."

"But I want to get another shot at that colt."

"Me too."

For the second time in two years, the Derby winner repaired to California, leaving the Triple Crown for some other horse, some other year. There were three weeks between the May 7 Derby and May 28 Preakness that year, and Nashua was greeted at Pimlico by a crowd still confident enough to send him off at 3-10. Saratoga was back on the scene, this time with Nick Shuk aboard, and since he last had seen Nashua in the Florida Derby, he had won the Chesapeake Stakes and finished a close second to Dedicate in the Jersey Stakes. Saratoga was second choice at almost 7-1 for the $100,000-added Preakness at one and three-sixteenths miles. The improving Traffic Judge, the Withers Stakes winner, was third choice at 17-2 in a field of eight. Horses of that ilk were among those that eventually would add even more to the glitter of a foal crop that could boast Nashua, Swaps, and Summer Tan.

Saratoga set the pace in the Preakness, and after a
half-mile in :47 1/5, there were two longshots and
nearly three lengths between himself and Nashua.
Perhaps mentally revved this time to pay extra attention to a high-class colt alone on the lead, Arcaro
nudged Nashua up a length closer in the next quarter-
mile, but Saratoga was full of run after six furlongs in
1:11. In the stretch, Nashua — again realizing it was no
time to be a playboy — set down for his best work. It
was needed. Saratoga fought back, and although the
chart showed him in front after a mile in 1:35 3/5, it
was only by a head.

Nashua's history and ancestry were laid on the line,
and the throbbing potency within emerged. He would not
lose. The son of Belair edged painfully and manfully into
a safer lead, which continued to grow slowly. Nashua hit
the wire a length in front of Saratoga, and his time of 1:54
3/5 set a new stakes and track record. Belair Stable, and
Mr. Fitz, had their first classic winner since 1939.

The time cut more than a second off Tom Fool's previous track mark, and the strength of the front pair was
emphasized by the seven-length margin the runner-up,
Saratoga, had on third-placed Traffic Judge. The adroit

Nance's Lad finished fourth, a neck off Traffic Judge.

Arcaro had no reservations, or quibbles, with the concentration, class, or professionalism of Nashua that time. "I would like to get one more crack at that horse Swaps," he declared. "He can't beat Nashua when my horse runs like he did today."

The Belmont Stakes in 1955 came up only two weeks after the Preakness. At one and a half miles, the Belmont is the longest of the Triple Crown series and is often styled "the test of champions." More aptly, in American racing, it is the *final* test of a champion. A colt that can excel at one and a quarter miles or so and also win the Belmont is truly a well-rounded specimen; on the other hand, a horse that needs one and a half miles before he can show to best advantage is likely a bit of a specialist that will have trouble finding spots that favor him.

Through no fault of Nashua's, the Belmont was something of an anti-climax. The Derby winner was back home terrorizing the best in California; the Preakness runner-up was resting. Other three-year-olds such as Traffic Judge and future champion Dedicate had plenty to offer, but neither was in the line-up.

Nashua and Arcaro were 15-100 for the $100,000-added Belmont on June 11. In a field of eight, Portersville was second choice at 9-1, and nothing else was shorter than 12-1. The Belmont was not a race to generate an inordinate amount of action. The mutuel pool was $328,336, or nearly $30,000 less than was bet on the next race on the card that day. Still, it was the Belmont Stakes, and one can only imagine the growing sound and excitement as Eddie Arcaro — The Master — brought the big, glistening Nashua up to the gate in front of the stands, where the gate is perched for this event. The moments before the Belmont break are cherished for this unique aspect. In no other of the Triple Crown races is the start played out in clear view of such a large part of the crowd.

As was so common, Nashua outbroke the field. Arcaro had learned long before that, with the colt's tender mouth, it was best to give Nashua his head at the start. Also, in the Belmont, the quick start gave Arcaro the opportunity to survey the situation as he tucked his big "hawk" back in amongst the pretenders, as close or far from the pace as he thought appropriate. In the Belmont, he chose to park Nashua second as C. V.

Whitney's Little Dell had six furlongs of fame. This required 1:13 3/5, after which Nashua powered on with his own agenda. The horse had exasperated Arcaro in the past and had been labeled a playboy, but in the Belmont he carried those white silks and red dots as if an ambassador to history. Nashua made no mistakes as he strode to the front after a mile, lengthened to two and a half lengths after one and a quarter miles, and toured home in splendid isolation by nine lengths. The 38-1 Blazing Count was second, Portersville third.

He was not a horse that made a point of doing more than necessary, and this Belmont certainly did not summon any call of his native reserves. He was never asked for much and won under a hold. Still, the time of 2:29 was only four-fifths of a second off the stakes record of Count Fleet and Citation and one and two-fifths seconds off the track record of Bolingbroke. (We cannot conjure a more vivid description of the result than a boyhood memory of our local South Florida paper's treatment: Three separate photos of the first three horses, with the serial captions: "One picture isn't enough"..."To show how far"..."Nashua was in front.")

Mr. Fitz had his sixth Belmont, and so did Arcaro.

Although we all know the Triple Crown is a sequence that is recognized as testing the depths of a three-year-old's foundation, we also have been treated over the years to the realization that a few horses bounce out of this crucible as if they are not sure what the fuss is about. Nashua was one of these.

Fitzsimmons, with or without memories of Hanover, saw no reason to back off. Three weeks after the Belmont, Nashua was back under colors. Having run in a half-dozen six-figure races at three, Nashua was sent out next for the $50,000-added Dwyer Stakes at Aqueduct. This was the sixty-seventh running and was set for one and a quarter miles. The Dwyer in 1920 had been the truest test of Man o' War's career, when he was pressed by John P. Grier before drawing off in the final furlong. In Nashua's year, the Dwyer brought yet another meeting with Saratoga, and this time the Belair colt was giving away weight, 126 pounds to 122. The only other horse in the televised event was King Ranch's Mainlander, in at 114 pounds. Although it could be easily surmised who was the favorite, odds did not figure into the scenario since management chose to run the race as a betless exhibition.

It is hoped that the reader has recognized what a splendid three-year-old Mrs. Scott had in Saratoga. In addition to the excellent efforts against Nashua we have described, Saratoga had added a victory in the Leonard Richards Stakes since the Preakness.

While Nashua almost always broke on top — a bird off a limb, Atkinson had said — he had not been ridden of late as a front runner. Overwhelming challenges had marked his performances most often at three. In the Dwyer, however, Arcaro reverted to the colt's juvenile days and kept him right on the lead. In the Preakness, Saratoga had played "catch me if you can," and Nashua could; in the Dwyer, it was the other way around, but the result was the same. Nashua led from the start. Saratoga was no less true to his own innate breeding and quality than before, and he chased the Belair colors as far as he could. After a half-mile in :49 3/5, the margin was a half-length. After six furlongs in 1:13 4/5, Saratoga and jockey Nick Shuk were still right there. After a mile in 1:38 2/5, Nashua had slipped out to a one and a half-length lead.

In the final quarter-mile, the verse was over, and only the chorus remained. Nashua had Saratoga's number. He drew out under the mildest of urging and won like the commanding presence he was, a five-length victor. Mainlander trailed home forty lengths behind Saratoga according to the chart, but still recipient of $5,000 for third place for King Ranch. The winning time was 2:03 4/5. While this was more than two seconds over the track record, it should be related that in those days of whatever level of track maintenance prevailed, the last two Dwyer winners, champions High Gun and Native Dancer, had each taken 2:05 or more.

In 1930, Gallant Fox had followed up his Triple Crown sweep with the Dwyer and then the Arlington Classic in Chicago. A quarter-century later, Fitzsimmons sent Nashua toward the same target for his next challenge. The Arlington race in 1955 had been reduced from its earlier one and a quarter-mile days and was run at a mile — a testing and often confusing distance. The Classic came up only two weeks after the Dwyer, but even so, once Fitzsimmons had sent the colt to Chicago, he prescribed a serious five-furlong work only three days before the race.

Arcaro was up as Nashua rattled off the furlongs. The sense of power and speed must have been

beguiling, even for The Master. Granting that a horse might need a bit of sharpening for a mile race after all those one and one-eighth-mile to one and a half-mile tests, it is hard to believe Eddie and Fitz had in mind what Nashua did that day. Nashua took Arcaro darting around the turn and through the lane, and the clockers caught the five-furlong work in :56 3/5. This was not just fast; it was two-fifths of a second swifter than the prevailing world record at the time!

Even given Fitzsimmons' robust approach to training, had Nashua lost the Arlington Classic there surely would have been some reporters with the temerity to suggest the work had been too much, too fast, too close. As it turned out, Nashua won it, but Arcaro and the younger Fitzsimmons, assistant John, came away making remarks about even this dazzling Hercules being "not at his best." Sunny Jim was not amused.

Nashua was 3-10 for the $100,000-added Arlington Classic. He was facing six others, and he carried top weight of 126, giving from six to ten pounds to each of the others. The second choice was the 6-1 Impromptu. He was ridden by Bill Hartack and was owned by Harry Isaacs, who habitually named his horses with the same letter of his own surname — Intent, Intentionally, Isasmoothie, Isendu, Ifabody, among others. Impromptu spent a lot of the Arlington Classic looking like another "I" word — "Itoldyouso" — that afternoon.

Impromptu had won the seven-furlong Warren Wright Memorial two weeks earlier, and although Nashua broke sharply, Impromptu quickly took the early lead. Munchausen, Nashua's old friend from his three-year-old debut, was just off both for a quarter-mile. Impromptu then scooted out to a daylight lead. Whether dulled or distracted, or neither, Nashua let him open up two lengths after a half-mile in :45 3/5.

Two more furlongs slipped past, and they were nearing the stretch as Hartack and Impromptu hung up 1:09 3/5 for six furlongs. This bell-ringing fraction was within a second of Hill Gail's track record and was good for a four-length lead. "Well-nigh desperate" was Evan Shipman's phrase for the moment — from Nashua's perspective — in the volume of *The American Racing Manual* that reviewed 1955.

It is a very good soldier we are addressing here, however, and Nashua found the heart to leap out of the foxhole. He kicked in under Arcaro's urgent partnership and within a furlong had reduced the lead by seventy-five percent. Impromptu was giving in to reality, but Traffic Judge was not. For some months, this son of Alibhai had been developing into something closer and closer to the top rank for trainer Woody Stephens, and — given six pounds and a favorite forced to dizzying effort just to reach the lead — Traffic Judge sensed his moment. In the final furlong, the 25-1 Traffic Judge's charge from seventh made him a worrisome force, and it took considerable will as well as talent for Nashua to stave him off and win by a half-length. The time was 1:35 1/5, which was only four-fifths of a second away from the storied world record set at Arlington by Equipoise twenty-three years before. (By 1955, Equipoise's mark still stood as a track record, but Citation had the world mile record at 1:33 3/5.)

Mr. Fitz was quoted as saying that "people under-rated that second horse." Still, whether deep down he accepted comments that Nashua was tired or not, the colt was sent to Saratoga for a brief rest.

By the time Nashua next heard the call to the post, the stakes of fame and fortune would be raised to Olympian heights.

CHAPTER 5

The Great Match Race

T he natural August target for an Eastern stable with a crack three-year-old is the Travers Stakes. Had Fitzsimmons run Nashua in that one and a quarter-mile event at old Saratoga, it would have meant four weeks between races. As matters happened, it was announced by late July that Nashua's next race would instead be in one for which a growing swell of sentiment had long been fermenting. He was to meet Swaps in a match race.

After the Derby, Swaps had reeled off four more admirable stakes victories. He had been so prodigious as to defeat the previous year's Derby winner, Determine, as early as the June 11 Californian Stakes. On August 20, eleven days before the Match Race, Swaps tried a grass course for the first time, in the one and three-sixteenth-mile American Derby, and held off Traffic Judge by a length. Between the Arlington Classic and the American Derby, Traffic Judge had dropped a narrow decision to the gritty Saratoga in the Choice Stakes. As a horse who had recent form against both Nashua and Swaps, he was of special interest; while he had seemed almost able to menace Swaps, he had clearly threatened Nashua. This bit of form probably added to Swaps' role as the presumed favorite as the weeks before the match tediously unfolded.

Russ Harris has written often on the subject, and in 1991 for the *Racing Times*, he reported on a conversation he recently had had with Eddie Arcaro. In 1999, Harris retold that account for this book:

"Eddie said he and Don Ameche were having dinner at one of the top places in New York (El Morocco). They were talking about Nashua and Swaps, and after a while Ameche said, 'You keep saying you should have won the Derby. Do you believe Nashua could beat Swaps in a match race?' Arcaro said he told him, 'Sure, he's a better horse.' Ameche pointed across the room and said, 'Well, there's William Woodward at a table over there. Let's ask him about it.' Ameche and Arcaro put the idea to the owner, who, after asking Eddie if he felt strongly about it, said all right."

The race was organized for Benjamin Lindheimer's Washington Park in Chicago — $100,000 winner-take-all, at the Derby distance (one and a quarter miles) and under Derby weight (126 pounds.).

Ameche's roll as matchmaker — or rather matchracemaker — was not from left field. The suave stage and screen man was a long-time horse racing fan and had some horses of his own.

Counter to the popular versions retold over the years that Ameche was a key, Lindheimer's daughter, Marje Everett, in the year 2000 told the author that "Don Ameche had nothing to do with arranging the match race."

She recalled instead that the durable Chicago horseman Charlie Wacker III "was a director of one of our companies, and he knew Billy Woodward and introduced him to my father. My father did not know Billy very long, but became very fond of him."

At the same time, Mrs. Everett said, Swaps' team of Rex Ellsworth and Mesh Tenney were friends of the Lindheimers: "I think they were appreciative that my

father was very gracious to them, even before they were fashionable."

The connections of her father to the principals, Mrs. Everett recalled, allowed Washington Park to secure the event when many other tracks were seeking the unique attraction.

Fitzsimmons began training Nashua for speed, to such an extent that there was brusque comment that he was blowing the deal from the beginning.

Before Jimmy Breslin became an acerbic general New York columnist, he was an outstanding sportswriter. In 1962, his book about Fitzsimmons, *Sunny Jim*, was published by Doubleday & Co. While it is a very entertaining book, we have been circumspect about using it as a reference, for the simple reason that the volume in the Keeneland Library has a cryptic inscription on the flyleaf: "I fail to recognize the chief character in this 'comedy of errors.' "— James E. Fitzsimmons.

Still, Breslin's commentary on the training for the match race seems consistent with other reports. One colorful passage concerning a public workout between races at Saratoga appears to be an eyewitness Breslin account:

From the stable area, coming in the same way they bring a heavyweight champion into the ring, four grooms walked Nashua toward Mr. Fitz. Al Robertson led him. There was a groom named Chico and another one named Andy and exercise boy Bill McCleary. They all had towels and were waving them around Nashua to keep the flies away.

"The last time I saw anybody come in like this it was Dempsey getting into the ring at Chicago," somebody said to Mr. Fitz.

"Well, he's a nice horse and there's a lot of flies around here and I kind of like to treat a horse right," Mr. Fitz said. But he had a little smile. This is the big leagues, son, the smile said.

Arcaro was up that afternoon, and they elicited gasps from the crowd with the sheer flash of the workout.

Arcaro, Breslin said, was enthralled enough to say out loud: "Maybe that other horse is a super horse, like they say. If he is, then forget it. But if he's just another real good race horse, then he's going to have some time with this dude."

Russ Harris quoted Arcaro as even more confi-

dent: "When I dismounted, I said 'Nobody's gonna beat this horse!' "

In stressing speed at the start, Arcaro and Fitzsimmons were harking back in history, heeding a seventeen-year-old lesson. While it is true that not all modern two-horse races had unfolded identically, the one that stood out was the 1938 Pimlico Special. War Admiral had been the supposed speed horse, but it was Seabiscuit who had taken the track from the start, put the other horse off his game, and smote him.

Back in a time when most races were match races, the best horse at that particular skill was the champion. As racing evolved into larger fields, a veritable tapestry of racing styles, luck, pace, and track condition played important roles; the individual who was best at the intricacies of being a racehorse in that crucible was not necessarily the best at head-to-head, *mano a mano* bloodletting.

Arcaro and Fitzsimmons recognized that in the peculiar ring they were facing, though, the most blatant of paradoxes prevailed: A suicide pace was the safest course.

The Blood-Horse sent Dan Bowmar III to Chicago to cover the race.

"The horse players began arriving at 9 a.m.," he recorded. Special excursions from California had been arranged, and airlines had added flights from New York, while a special train from Louisville was put on. Bowmar and various other writers observed a baffling sense of nonchalance about it all in Chicago itself. Perhaps, local sportswriters felt the raucous horse crowd was infringing on the Cubs and White Sox. The national media, however, was caught up. Our own memories are of sitting entranced before the national television coverage and of evening network news leading with "East vs. West in Chicago."

Washington Park management exulted in its moment, but did not forget the basics of the racetrack business. As Bowmar reported, the first utterance from the public address system was: "Good afternoon, ladies and gentlemen. Welcome to Washington Park on this day of days in the history of American racing. Daily-double windows are located on the main floor..."

A crowd of 35,262 turned out, and while they had money in their pockets, their real interest in the match race itself was more a matter of pure sport than betting opportunity. Indeed, the mutuel pool on the Match

Race's win-betting-only was $174,737, smaller than the total pool of any other race on the card but the first. Overall, they bet $2.3 million on the day. On the most recent previous weekend, Saturday's crowd of 21,670 had bet $1.7 million.

A disheartening rain had visited the track in the days before. Arcaro had studied the track and noted a path that seemed better than others. It was a bit to the right of the inside post position, at least at the break. Since he was drawn on the inside, and there was an empty gate between the two falcons to facilitate a clean start, Arcaro had a better than usual opportunity to get to the best path early. The track condition had been updated from "slow" to "good" late in the afternoon, but it apparently was unrelentingly deep and testing beneath the surface.

Swaps was 3-10, Nashua 6-5.

While the prevailing images of the two horses, instilled by the Derby, was of Swaps as the speed horse and Nashua the inexorable stalker, Nashua had always had a great knack for bursting out of the gate. On August 31, 1955, Arcaro asked for perfection in that skill. Crashing his whip and his vocal chords in unison, the Master reverted to being an apprentice on a half-mile gyp track. "You have to come out of there 'Whoop-de-doing,' " an ex-rider on such a bullring once said, and Arcaro the winner of classics morphed into a great half-miler, if just for the moment.

Nashua swerved right at Arcaro's urging, and Swaps swerved right, too. Nashua established his place in the preferred spot, and from that moment on he had an advantage. "Keep Swaps busy," Fitzsimmons had told Arcaro. "You should be all right."

For the occasion, *Daily Racing Form* recorded some interim furlongs as well as the more normal chart fractions. Nashua went the first eighth-mile in twelve seconds. The next he went in eleven. The old drills back at Saratoga had come to fruition. A quarter-mile in :23 had him in front by a length or so. Shoemaker tried several times to move Swaps to him, but Nashua each time had the answer. This was a powerful animal that day, and every good card just floated across the table into the hand of the chortling Arcaro.

After a half-mile in :46, Nashua still had his length lead. Swaps moved to be lapped on him. Nashua darted the next furlong in twelve seconds, for a :58 for the first

five-eighths. Still, only a half-length separated East and West after six furlongs in 1:10 2/5. If the nation had envisioned a throb to the wire, this seemed to set it off.

But Nashua rebuffed Swaps and slipped away to a one and a half-length lead after a mile. It was role reversal from Churchill Downs, the chestnut closing on the bay only to see the bay kick in again and draw out. The seventh furlong Nashua had clicked out in :13 1/5, for a fraction of 1:23 3/5. The next furlong took fourteen seconds, but the damage was done. Actually, as is true in many a front-running race, the damage was done to both, but it was the survivor in front by that one and a half-length margin after a mile in 1:37 3/5.

By midstretch, Nashua had increased his lead only to two lengths. That he had gained only a half-length more on Swaps although upping his speed to thirteen seconds for that furlong was testimony to the grit of the other colt — and perhaps a puzzle to work with later as reports of Swaps' lameness began to spread.

After nine furlongs in 1:50 3/5, Nashua had it won. Swaps wavered over toward the rail, but that only put him in the deeper going as Nashua continued on the favored and savored path. A final furlong — still punc-

tuated by Eddie the wide-eyed apprentice-imperson-
ator bringing down the occasional reminder — took
:13 3/5. Nashua pulled out to win by six and a half
lengths in 2:04 1/5. Swaps fans later pointed out that it
was awfully slow for their horse to have lost in, but it
was also pretty slow for Nashua to have won in. The
track condition, and the tactics, must have been
exceedingly wearying. Shoemaker had done the prop-
er thing and eased Swaps a bit before the wire when he
recognized futility.

Young Woodward was the sporting hero, Arcaro the
heaving champ — "I'm more tired than Nashua" —
Fitzsimmons the old man fending off too many well-mean-
ing hugs and smearing cheek kisses, and the Nasrullah—
Segula colt was clearly the Horse of the Year. And at the
Fitzsimmons barn back in New York? Well, why ask?

In Lindheimer's penthouse, Bowmar recorded the
stoic comments of Ellsworth. Always rather a gaunt
figure, Ellsworth must have seemed downright spectral
as he gamely faced the prospect of discussing his deep
and recent hurt for public consumption: "It's hard to
say what happened. It will take a while to decide what
was wrong. We know the horse didn't run his race, and

if you know the horse didn't run his race, you know something is wrong."

Ellsworth stressed that Nashua's taking the lead was not a surprise, nor had it been immediately worrisome in itself, since Swaps had won coming from behind on earlier occasions.

Bowmar also recorded a brief statement from owner Woodward, "who had been leaning against a desk in a corner of the room." Woodward sounded like a pretty adept racetracker, as well as a sportsman trying to be reserved: "Our riding instructions were to go the front if possible, except that we didn't add the 'if possible.' I don't know where people got the idea that Nashua doesn't have early speed. He always has been quick from the gate. Normally, we don't send him to the front because we have several horses in a race. Today, we had only one horse to beat...

"We would be happy to meet Swaps again, but not in a match race. It is too difficult to arrange the details for a match race. We were lucky this time."

By the next morning, it was being questioned whether Swaps and his camp had been the opposite — unlucky. Since before the Derby it had been widely known that Swaps had been nagged by a stone bruise, which Tenney had coped with by use of a leather pad and sponge between plate and hoof. The day after the match race it was reported that Swaps had been lame. As these stories are apt to do, it grew as it spread. Many years later, Shoemaker wrote in the book with Barney Nagler:

> Word got out that the morning of the race, Swaps could hardly get out of the stall...He had an infection in his right front foot, and when Mesh Tenney put him through a work the day before the race, he put a leather pad around the bad foot to protect it. The track came up muddy, after a heavy rain, and some mud got up inside the leather pad and made the infection worse.
>
> Mesh Tenney went to see Ben Lindheimer... Mr. Lindheimer... told Mesh that he couldn't call the race off; too much was involved...I think Ellsworth and Tenney thought Swaps could handle the situation even with a bad foot. When I was warming Swaps up before the race, I felt that his action wasn't right, but I thought it was because the

track was muddy in spots.

This was obviously something Shoemaker has been asked about often, and that story of thirty-three years after the fact was consistent with his commentary in the 1976 book with Dan Smith.

Reaching back to 1955, contemporary comments attributed to the Swaps camp spoke either of a stable without a problem, a stable with an excuse, or a stable grappling with what to say in public.

Bill Boniface of the *Baltimore Sun* reported he had been told that Swaps was dead lame. On the other hand, that same morning, Tenney read a prepared statement: "It is a well-known fact that this horse first injured his right front foot early in his three-year-old career and prior to any of his major races this year. He has been sound in every race in which he was started in 1955, including yesterday's race with Nashua."

Mrs. Everett's recollection was that the difficulties "brought out the class in all the parties involved...On the morning of the race, I was in my father's office and Rex Ellsworth and Mesh Tenney came in and told him that Swaps had some soreness. They had him standing in cold water, and they kept tubbing Swaps, and I think it was a joint decision to go on with the race. Billy Woodward knew about it. The race was on television, so that was a complication."

Evan Shipman later quoted Dr. Warren Skinner, state veterinarian for Illinois, as having seen Swaps walking on the racetrack on the morning after the race. Although he stipulated he did not examine the colt, Dr. Skinner described his walking action as apparently sound. This was observed, Shipman said, about an hour after Ellsworth allegedly had told Boniface the horse was lame.

Of this tiny scene in the big picture, we are left wondering: What is tougher to believe — that a horse would go to the track instead of just walking under the shed the day after a grinding one and a quarter-mile race or that a state racetrack veterinarian could confuse the identity of a horse so much in his own local limelight for a number of days?

On August 28, Shipman's column in *Daily Racing Form* had quoted Fitzsimmons at some length. There was confidence and satisfaction in Sunny Jim's remarks, although after the fact they seemed invested of an enormous irony:

"He (Fitzsimmons) emphasized his respect for the brilliant California colt...and also his admiration for Ellsworth and Tenney, saying 'those boys really know their business, and I have a high regard for both of them...What I like best about this race is that both colts are coming up to it in shape to do perfect justice to themselves. Ordinarily, I don't like match races. Never have. So often they make for bad feeling, and something goes wrong with one horse or the other. Then, if you don't go, you are accused of ducking the other fellow, and if you do go, and get beaten, why there are excuses. And nobody likes to have to make excuses. But this time, I feel differently about it. Nashua is good, maybe better than he was in Kentucky. Swaps is good. I've just been down to have a look at him. That fast work he had yesterday morning could not have hurt him a bit. If it had hurt Swaps, that big chestnut would not be showing the condition that he does."

After the hubbub had begun, Tower of *Sports Illustrated* quoted Ellsworth in his bewilderment: "If I had an alibi for this race, which I don't, I'd feel a lot better." On the other hand, a few paragraphs earlier, Tower had quoted Ellsworth as saying, Swaps "made three tries, trying to run, but it was stinging him so bad."

So much did the Nashua-Swaps race engender emotions — from the sporting press as well as from proponents — that we cannot describe any discovered reference as objective. Appropriately, the strongest comment came from the most closely involved, as in Fitzsimmons' later summary that "I think Nashua can beat Swaps doing anything."

Whatever Swaps' true condition was, or whatever the agendas were of the various individuals who made statements about it, one irony was that it was the loser's status that would thereafter climb. The following year, Swaps won eight of ten races. Nashua had twelve more races left in his career after the match race and won seven.

At four, Swaps convinced the world of his greatness, and his fans took as gospel that he was the better horse. He was molten bronze and sunlight as he dazzled through a series of world records that harked back to Man o' War.

It was Shoemaker himself who eventually tempered the super-horse talk. Twenty-one years later, in the book written with Smith, Shoe conjectured that, "I don't know if Swaps could have won the Triple Crown or not. As a guess, maybe he could have beaten Nashua in the Preakness…but I'm not sure he could have gone a good mile and a half against a top horse like Nashua on a track like Belmont. Swaps never did impress me as a top distance horse. He was a real good horse, a great one, but only at certain distances…I think a mile and one-quarter was about Swaps' maximum effective distance."

For 1956, Swaps would be Horse of the Year, and Nashua and Swaps never met again.

On the afternoon of August 31, 1955, however, the hand-wringing and angst-ringing were but a whisper.

"Vindication," Arcaro would say for years. "It vindicated what I kept saying after the Kentucky Derby: Nashua would have won the Derby and the Triple Crown if I hadn't screwed up by watching Summer Tan and let Shoe steal an easy lead on Swaps. You couldn't let Shoe take an easy lead on anything."

The tousled old gentleman in the rough-hugging winner's circle, Sunny Jim, would look back, sift through many a scene, and say fondly that it was, "the moment of a lifetime."

CHAPTER 6

Honor, Glory — And Death

Nashua's very next race after the great Chicago victory brought him up short with a slap. He took on older horses for the first time, and a crack field it was. Arcaro undoubtedly had heard all his life that it was axiomatic that a good older horse would generally beat a good younger horse, even with the weight-for-age scale, but he stuck with the younger Nashua. The race was the Sysonby, which had been a mile race, but had been lengthened by Belmont Park management to one and one-eighth miles. The purse was doubled to $100,000, both changes made in the hope of attracting another meeting with Swaps. The date was September 24, or three and a half weeks after the Washington Park showdown. Swaps would not run again that season, but his absence hardly made the Sysonby assignment easier.

Robert Kleberg Jr. of King Ranch never backed off from facing a champion. (In 1973, he showed us through his stable and pointed to a big three-year-old, No Bias, who he hoped might meet Secretariat later that year. Instead it was another of his homebreds, Prove Out, a few stalls away, that would lower Secretariat's colors, in the Woodward, but the King Ranch horse had been sold by then.) In 1955, Kleberg had fired some meek shots at Nashua — with a 63-1 shot named Retamero in the Belmont and with Mainlander in the Dwyer. For the Sysonby, though, he had his big gun — High Gun.

The distinction between a good horse, a champion, and a "great horse" is always hazy. High Gun apparently has been put down in history as on the south side of great, but surely not by much. In 1954, he had won the Belmont Stakes and the three-year-old championship, and in 1955, he had jousted with a strong division, especially Helioscope, at an exalted level of handicap weights — winning under 130 and 132 pounds.

Arcaro had ridden High Gun in five straight races. Bill Boland replaced him for the Sysonby. Despite the severity of the challenge, Nashua was made the 3-5 favorite. Helioscope was less than 4-1, with High Gun at 9-2, Jet Action 6-1, and Mr. Turf, the lone longshot, at 31-1. A footnote to the race was that three of the horses had each won at Belmont on the afternoon of October 9, 1954, almost a year before. On that date, Nashua had won his Futurity, High Gun had won the Manhattan Handicap, and Jet Action took an allowance race. For the Sysonby, Nashua as the only three-year-old carried 121 pounds by the scale, the others 126. The track was sloppy.

All in the field save High Gun set off in a dazzling four-horse duel. After a quarter-mile, Nashua was in front of Helioscope by a head in :22 3/5, with Jet Action only another head behind and Mr. Turf a similar margin back in fourth. High Gun already trailed by seven, so seemingly in another world that, as Kleberg recalled years later, "I had a bunch of friends with me, and I told them 'quit watching my horse. I don't know what happened to him, but it's a good race in front.' "

Actually, it was a death match in front. The torrid duel continued, and after a half-mile Mr. Turf had a length lead in :45 1/5. After six furlongs, it was the accomplished Jet Action with a head in front of

Helioscope, Nashua third, and Mr. Turf fading, and the fraction was 1:10 1/5.

Meanwhile, Boland had waited patiently, and High Gun was only four lengths back. The mile was reached in 1:36. For a three-year-old to have contested a front-running duel in which one of the first to give in was Helioscope — Suburban Handicap under 128, Monmouth Handicap under 131— ordinarily would have clinched a notable triumph. For Nashua, however, this distinction did little but reduce the number of his assailants. Jet Action — a son of Kentucky Derby winner Jet Pilot and Horse of the Year Busher — was a very good horse, and it was he who made the younger colt weaken (hardly a phrase familiar to Nashua's followers). Jet Action had two lengths on Nashua at the eighth pole, but then in the final furlong, High Gun completed his lengthy rally on the outside just in time to beat Jet Action by a head. The final time was 1:49 1/5. Nashua was beaten two lengths and had more than three on Helioscope.

High Gun thus clinched the title as champion older horse.

Nashua came back for the conclusion of his three-year-old campaign three weeks later, on October 15. The race was the $75,000-added Jockey Club Gold Cup, then secure in its status as a two-mile test of endurance unmatched by other American races of comparable splendor. The Belmont strip was again sloppy. The crowd seemed to have no fear that the track condition was the worry for Nashua, for he was sent off at 1-4. He tracked the high-class Thinking Cap for about half the race, then strode confidently to the front and gradually increased his margin. He won by five lengths in 3:24 4/5.

Arcaro had him well in hand as he won from Thinking Cap, who had fifteen lengths on third-placed Mark's Puzzle. Chevation, the only older horse in the race, was fourth, and Sweet Chariot was last. The three-year-olds carried 119, Chevation 124.

Thus ended the second championship season in two years for Belair Stud's Nashua. He had won ten of twelve races, and his earnings of $752,550 were the highest ever for any horse in a single year. Although Horse of the Year honors were not officially conferred for some weeks, it was obvious that the title would be bestowed upon him, which in due course it was. Those

articulating *Daily Racing Form*'s and sister publication *Morning Telegraph*'s free handicap for three-year-olds shrugged, or choked; they put 130 pounds on both Nashua and Swaps.

For the fifth time in his career, Sunny Jim Fitzsimmons was the leading trainer in earnings. His total of $1,270,055 included not only Nashua's record, but the major success of two Wheatley Stable fillies as well. High Voltage, the champion two-year-old filly for Mr. Fitz in 1954, came back to win the Coaching Club American Oaks, but then Wheatley's other star, Misty Morn, emerged later in the year to secure the three-year-old filly honors for 1955. Belair Stud, which had led the owners' list for the founder in 1939, was narrowly edged by Hasty House Farms for leading owner in 1955 — $832,879 to $831,425.

Nashua's talents were widely honored, although his idiosyncrasies were never ignored. Stated Joe Estes, editor of *The Blood-Horse*, in *American Race Horses of 1955*: "Nashua…was a playboy who found distraction in everything…He played cat-and-mouse with opponents when he might have whaled the daylights out of them…rarely concentrated his full energies on the task at hand." At the

same time, he embodied "an approach to physical perfection and perhaps was endowed with more brute
strength than any 3-year-old since Man o' War."

The compelling and lusty physical being that had
enthralled William Faulkner was admired as well by the
Daily Racing Form's linguistic curmudgeon, Charles Hatton:

"Nashua's development is so pronounced that even the
layman, seeing him come into the paddock, recognizes at
once he is a horse of exceptional strength and character, a
magnetic personality among those of his kind."

Hatton pegged Nashua at the end of his three-year-
old season at 16.1 hands tall at the withers. He, plus
Fitzsimmons — indeed the world — might lament that
Nashua's ears were a bit low on the poll and sometimes
were displayed at a rather casual half-mast. This, however, was a trait that was easily traced to his broodmare
sire, Johnstown, and so could hardly be seen as a fault
other than aesthetically. Otherwise, Nashua's head was
handsome, the jowl bold, and the eye intelligent.

Hatton continued:

> The champion has good rein length and a
> neck somewhat more heavily crested than that
> of the average colt of his years. The neck

extends gracefully and almost imperceptibly into strong, well developed withers which in turn seem to range well into his back. This, together with a slightly arching loin and the abnormal muscular investiture across his hips, come to exceptional power for carrying high weights big distances...Seen from above, in the stands, he appears to be two horses wide. He weighs more than 1,200 pounds, which exceeds the weight of many retired stallions.

...Nashua girths a full 72 inches, and his ribs are well sprung, affording ample room for heart and lungs. He had never been thought wanting in either...The Horse of the Year has a long pelvis and the sloping croup character- istic of Nasrullah, Nearco, Dante and others of his male line.

Nashua's underpinning is a study, really something to inspire a sculptor. His legs are as unblemished as when he was foaled...Though the champion has tremendous substance bod- ily, his legs are those of a stayer. The muscles are long, strong and supple, without any of the exaggerated development to be noted in the one-dimensional sprinters...

The hind legs are fairly straight and there is evident drive in the long muscles of the gaskins, which seem to extend directly into the hock...At a glance, Nashua's legs are those of the classic horse...

It is interesting that Arcaro says he has never ridden a horse having a smoother way of moving. And in this connection we recall that Sir Gordon Richards said that in his opinion Nasrullah had the most facile extended action of any of the many horses he rode in his 26 years as England's leading jockey.

Evan Shipman had chimed in with additional praise of Nashua's underpinning: "Take a close look at Nashua's legs, and you will see a trainer's ideal; hard, flat bone, and clean fluted tendons."

Two weeks after the Jockey Club Gold Cup, the idyll of Nashua's world, circa 1955, was shattered by gunfire. William Woodward Jr.'s wife shot and killed her husband in their Long Island home. The prominence of the Woodwards, socially as well as in sports, assured tremendous press coverage. Indeed, the Woodward affair took on a life of its own, resurfacing many years later in the form of the Dominick Dunne novel and television show, *The Two Mrs. Grenvilles*. The death was ruled accidental, there having been burglaries recently in the couple's neighborhood.

Although the death, of course, was a human tragedy that exceeded racing, it is the career of Nashua we are addressing here. Inevitably, it was a major sports story, too. (We personally recall the *Fort Lauderdale Daily News* headline, front page — not sports page — and the identity given even there was Woodward as Nashua's owner.)

A few weeks after the death, A. B. (Bull) Hancock Jr., head of Claiborne Farm, offered to the executors of the estate that he would manage the Belair Thoroughbred operation for ten years, or until William Woodward III turned twenty-one. Maintenance of a great name in Thoroughbred racing was not the uppermost thought in the minds of the executors, however. After all, the estate of the senior Woodward had not yet been settled. The historic stable, and the broodmare band of some two dozen, were to be sold.

Humphrey S. Finney, for many years a charming and knowledgeable character in the Thoroughbred auction world, addressed the sale in a chapter of his book *Fair Exchange*, written with Raleigh Burroughs (Charles Scribner's Sons, New York, 1974). Finney, president of the Fasig-Tipton Thoroughbred auction house, had appraised the elder Woodward's stock. He was called in again for an appraisal, as was Hancock, at whose Claiborne Nashua was quartered for a tense couple of months while all the plans were made. Finney recognized that no horse of the established fame and status of Nashua ever had been offered for auction. To hold down on collusion and crank bids, he recommended the horse be sold by sealed bids, and ten percent down was required for a bid to be recognized. The rest of the stock was divided into two major groups, mares/weanlings and racehorses/yearlings. Finney thought they should be sold by regular open-bidding auction, but the accountants and bankers who were executors liked the sealed bid motif for each division.

At the appointed hour at the Hanover Bank, 11 a.m. on December 15, the bids were opened. It was two and a half months since Woodward's death. One bid on

Nashua that was to have almost as much attention as the winning bid was for $24.03, tendered by a twelve-year-old named Karen Ann McGuire and described as her "life savings." She may have dreamt of Nashua, but stipulated she was willing to take any horse no one else wanted. (A group of Hanover officers went together to buy her a horse from a less exalted source.)

Finney had evaluated Nashua alone at $1,200,000, which would mean the first million-dollar one-horse sale. He had recommended such a range to Stavros Niarchos, but the shipping mogul could not get past the fact that the great European horse Tulyar had only brought $700,000 in recent years.

"There were eleven bids on Nashua, five of them over $1,000,000," Finney wrote. It was the financial equivalent of, say, the Wood Memorial. Leslie Combs II, associated with John W. Hanes and Christopher Devine, et al., put in the winning bid at $1,251,200, which did not beat by much the bid of Lou Doherty at $1,226,084. Doherty, owner of a Kentucky stallion operation, was backed by William du Pont Jr. At an even $1,200,000 was the bid of Elmendorf Farm owner Maxwell Gluck, bidding on his own.

Many years later, Combs recalled for *The New York Times* that "a lot of people have asked me over the years how I came up with that odd figure. It was simple, really. I thought the horse would probably bring about $1,250,000, and I added another 1 and a 2 at the end of that figure to top an even bid." Others in the syndicate, in addition to Devine and Hanes, were Walter J. Salmon, P. A. B. Widener III, Harry M. Warner, and Robert W. McIlvain.

A few months later, the group headed by Mildred Woolwine, which had bought the mares, consigned them to the Keeneland auction ring in Kentucky. Segula, carrying a full sibling to Nashua, was purchased by Niarchos for $126,000, then a world record for a mare. (She produced only that foal for Niarchos. Named Stavroula, Nashua's full sister failed to win, then produced the French stakes winner Wittgenstein and New Love, the dam of American Derby winner Determined King.)

Leslie Combs II owned Spendthrift Farm near Lexington. He was already recognized as a keen salesman, a Bluegrass entrepreneur who had pioneered the modern technique of syndicating a horse into thirty-two shares or so, to spread the risk. His Spendthrift consignments were displayed amid mint juleps and country ham and biscuits in front of the white columns of his grand old home. Then, at the Keeneland July sales, they often fetched top dollar. Having Nashua would move Spendthrift to a whole new category of glamour, as well as quality.

Combs announced immediately that Nashua would remain in training at four. With career earnings of $945,415, he was only one major win from becoming the second racehorse ever to earn $1 million. The first, Citation, had earned $1,085,760, so the leading money-earning record appeared not too far in the distance.

Another key part of Combs' immediate announcement was that Nashua would once again rejoin the stable of Sunny Jim Fitzsimmons.

Some things had changed. Death had intruded with its indifference and haughtiness. "I was thirty-one years with those (Belair) colors, and it's going to be different," Fitzsimmons mused. "It can't help but be different. I don't even know who half the new owners are."

Still, the precious animal had been returned to his care, so the glory road beckoned anew.

NASHUA

CHAPTER 7

The Last Campaign

N ashua, High Voltage, and Misty Morn were part of one of the most valuable trainloads of horses ever sent along the railways of America. At stops in small communities, the curious would come out, hoping to get a glimpse of this near-mythical horse they had read about: "Which one's Nashuway?"

The train proceeded to Hialeah, the winter palace of sport and elegance that had hosted royalty in its clubhouse as well as on its racetrack. The $100,000-added Widener Handicap at one and a quarter miles was the centerpiece of the Hialeah meeting for older horses and had been since Columbiana and War Admiral won the second and third runnings in 1937 and 1938. It was Nashua's target, of course. In the meantime, the ante had been upped, and Combs had turned down the quick profit from an offer of $1,500,000 to take Nashua off his hands.

Just as had happened the previous winter, weather and track conditions confounded Mr. Fitz' hope to get in a prep race. Many years beyond the claptrap days of the turn of the century, Mr. Fitz did not like to run or work a horse over an unfavorable track if he could avoid it. Now, he had added more pressure to his own task by deciding to send out this vaunted star into the Widener, in his first attempt for a new owner, off works alone.

In a strategy that would leave many present-day trainers — not to mention owners — with mouths agape, Fitzsimmons vanned Nashua from Hialeah to another South Florida track, Tropical Park, because he thought the going there was a bit firmer. Mr. Fitz worked him the entire one and a quarter-mile distance of the Widener. It was only four days before the race itself!

Ted Atkinson was up for the work, which attracted a crowd of about 500, although the Tropical Park meeting had closed a number of weeks earlier. It had been four months since he last raced, but Nashua had been honed to a Menuhin pitch by the clever old concert master. If there was any remaining rust, it was blown away by an opening quarter-mile in :22 2/5. Nashua proceeded to better some Tropical distance records en route to a complete clocking of 2:01 4/5. This would have been good enough to have won all but two runnings of the Widener. (It was faster than the closest thing Tropical had to one and a quarter-mile races, the configuration of the track and chute dictating a race distance sixty-one feet short of the full route; the workout ended on a turn.)

Widener Day, February 18, 1956, arguably was the apogee of the glory that was Hialeah. The crowd of 42,366 was a record for the track. For once, the handicap star overshadowed even the glamour of the new classic crop starting along the trail to the Kentucky Derby. The next week, the crowd attracted there to see the budding Florida-bred star Needles win the Flamingo Stakes was nearly 10,000 fewer. That just a glimpse of Nashua was the lure of many on Widener Day was evidenced by the betting on the two Saturdays. The $2.78 million wagered on all of Widener Day was less than $200,000 over the total that the considerably smaller crowd bet on the Flamingo card.

The task Nashua was facing was exceptional. That he faced it off works alone lent the event such drama

that it stood as a beacon in the career of his trainer —
he so often associated with the opposite approach of
racing horses into prime fitness. In his first handicap,
Nashua had been assigned 127 pounds. He was giving
six pounds each to Social Outcast and El Chama, eight
to Sailor, and thirteen to Find.

These were horses near the top drawer. Social
Outcast was Alfred Vanderbilt's stretch-runner extraor-
dinaire, whose sweeps from behind accomplished tri-
umphs in a dozen major races. He and stablemate Find
were lingering reminders of the magic of Vanderbilt's
1950 foal crop, which also had included Native Dancer.

Find, by Discovery, was a stellar stakes horse in his
own right, owning thirteen major stakes victories. At
six, when Nashua met him frequently, Find was at the
height of his ruggedness. He won three important
handicaps that year and placed in no fewer than thirteen others. He had speed, almost always ran his race,
and in this Widener was the dangerous lead jab in a
Vanderbilt combination of punches.

Brookmeade Stable's Sailor had won the Toboggan
and Fall Highweight Handicaps, both sprints, but also
had stretched out to win both the Roamer and the

Pimlico Special the previous autumn. Even some of the longshots in that nine-horse Widener field were distinguished. El Chama, although 29-1, had won the previous year's Washington, D.C., International. Sea O Erin, 21-1, was a winner of fifteen stakes, and several of his best moments had come at Hialeah, while Jamie K. was remembered for his neck losses in the Preakness and Belmont Stakes to none other than Native Dancer. Although well past his prime at six, the 34-1 Jamie K. was still intriguing, especially since he was in receipt of twenty-two pounds from Nashua!

Despite the layoff, the weights, and the quality of his field, Nashua was sent off at a sentiment-directed 2-5. He won it, but it took one of those races that emphasized a courageous streak that countered his stubborn streak. (In the nine close finishes in his career, Nashua prevailed in eight, the exception being the bump-and-lean finish of the Cherry Hill in his third race at two.)

Sports Illustrated, as so often was the case in the great horse's career, captured the drama under the Royal Palms of Hialeah: "Nashua Was Crying To Run" was the headline for its report, and in an era before instant color photography was so routine, the weekly maga-

zine commissioned a color illustration of Nashua and Eddie Arcaro — in the blue and orange silks he would wear at four.

Sea O Erin broke first, but Atkinson hustled Find out to take a swift lead. The jockey's task had been to help hone Nashua to his best earlier that week, but now his assignment was to help orchestrate Nashua's defeat. True professional that he was, Atkinson made a fine attempt to do just that, and it almost worked. Nashua broke third and was in that same spot after a half-mile in :46 3/5. Find led by a head over Sea O Erin at that point, and the Vanderbilt pacemaker edged out to a daylight lead after six furlongs in 1:10 4/5. Nashua was then fourth, but less than two lengths behind. After another quarter-mile, Find still held the lead, with a testing 1:35 3/5 for a mile, but big Nashua had loomed up beside him and was only a half-length behind. Not only was Find still full of vinegar, but by then Bill Hartack had brought Sailor up into the fray. The Brookmeade colt slid in between Find on the rail and Nashua and was a head back in third. Eric Guerin had begun his run from last on Social Outcast, who was boiling up in fourth.

If the phrase "blanket finish" had not been invented years before, it would have burst into the lexicon of the Turf that day in Florida. Onward surged the steaming foursome. No one could separate himself from the others. The battle raged. Only precious seconds remained for the decision, and still no one set himself apart from the heaving sides of his antagonists. There was nothing remotely comfortable about this battle now. The final furlong required :26 2/5. In such circumstances, prodigal speed and energy have long since been wasted. Only courage, and resolve, remain. It is difficult to assign to any of this four-in-hand a shortage of either, and yet it was one horse, Nashua, who thrust his head to the wire, similar to his Wood Memorial triumph. Side views from the ground show Nashua clearly a neck in front, if only for an opportune moment, but the official margin was a head. Social Outcast registered next, a head in front of Sailor, while Find was still only another neck away.

The final time was 2:02. This clocking was a full second over the track and stakes record and therefore stands as a testament to how little comparative final times can mean in horse races. The record was held by

El Mono. Put El Mono in a vote for excellence against any of the blooded Widener foursome of 1956, and we doubt he'd get a look.

So, Nashua, who had first crossed the million-dollar threshold in horse dealing, had now become the second to cross it in horse racing.

His next race would come four Saturdays later. A frustrating aspect of Nashua's career was that his most glamorous victories were followed by defeats: After the Wood Memorial came the Derby; after the Match Race came the Sysonby, and after the Widener came the most stunning defeat of all.

In comments to the National Press Club in Washington, D.C., later that year, Arcaro put into words what a few Turf writers had conjectured before, i.e., that Nashua "didn't like to get dirt in his face." The $100,000-added Gulfstream Park Handicap, the colt's second race at four, perhaps was an example. After two years of being so quick out of the gate that race charts often placed him first at the start, Nashua at four only twice would be recorded as getting away first. In the Gulfstream Park Handicap, he was facing a field roughly equal to that of the Widener, and the weights and spread had gone upward. He was assigned 129 pounds, again going one and a quarter miles. Sailor, who had been beaten two heads while in receipt of eight pounds at Hialeah, was now getting ten pounds. Find again got thirteen pounds, and one of those developing campaigners who lend hope to many an owner, Mielleux, was getting nineteen pounds. Wise Margin, yet another of the high-class handicap horses of the time, was in receipt of sixteen pounds, and Jet Action — despite his finish ahead of Nashua at scale weights the previous September — was getting four pounds.

The crowd flocked to Nashua, but a certain reality crept into the handicapping. After being 2-5 in the Widener, he was 7-10 at Gulfstream. He got away third, was fifth after a half-mile, and no doubt got plenty of dirt kicked at him. Hartack put Sailor on the lead, and he turned back Find after a sterling duel of more than a mile and skittered home by one and three-quarters lengths in 2:00 3/5. Mielleux came along to beat the avid Vanderbilt horse for second. Nashua, meanwhile, was clearly in trouble by the far turn, and although Arcaro got into him early, he never made an impression and finished fifth, beaten seven lengths.

Arcaro was dumbfounded, and Fitzsimmons had to summon a great deal of personal history to mutter the standard line, "That's horse racing."

Sailor went on to win the John B. Campbell Handicap in his next race, that Maryland race having been seen at one point — idealistically no doubt — as a possible vehicle for another meeting of Nashua and Swaps. (The latter returned to action some months after a portion of his bothersome hoof had been cut away and allowed to grow back.)

If Nashua's last two breaks had not seemed on par with so many of his earlier thrusts from the gate, his next start was close to a disaster. Almost two months had passed since the Gulfstream debacle, and the stable had returned to New York. On May 5, Nashua was saddled for the one and one-eighth-mile Grey Lag Handicap, a $50,000-added event at Jamaica. It was Kentucky Derby Day at Churchill Downs. Arcaro, having won a record five Derbys, felt he should be there, and although his mount, Head Man, was not even demonstrably the stronger half of the C. V. Whitney entry, The Master chose the Run for the Roses.

Atkinson once again deputized. The assignment was

a typically demanding one for Nashua. The weight assignment was still high, 128 pounds, and the infuriating Find was right there again, this time getting ten pounds. Two other stout handicappers appeared on the scene as well, each getting eight pounds from Nashua. These were Fisherman and Joe Jones. Fisherman had lost by only a neck to High Gun in the Belmont Stakes of two years previous, and in 1954 he had become the first American winner of the Washington, D.C., International. Like Find, he was a model of ruggedness, and the eleven stakes he won also included the Champagne, Travers, and Lawrence Realization. Perhaps even tougher in one sense was Joe Jones, who made 175 starts, and of the thirty-four he won, ten were good-class stakes.

Against this quality, and coming off a dismal defeat and a long layoff, Nashua was barely odds-on at 95-100.

Nashua, so often sure-footed and quick at the break, went to his knees. Atkinson gathered him up and stayed aboard. If dirt in his face made him cantankerous, this clumsy start perhaps just made him mad. Nashua trailed by three lengths as Cavort made a brave run to the front early, with Find second. Find then

surged to the front, and Nashua tagged along with him. After six furlongs, Atkinson had moved the favorite to the front, and he went head and head with Find for the rest of the way. Fisherman joined them in the stretch from his contending position, and for the second time in three races, Nashua was in the midst of a blanket finish. The three horses hit the wire almost together, but the "almost" was significant: Nashua again willed his way to victory. He scored by a head over Find, who had a head on Fisherman. The time was 1:50 3/5, compared to the track record of 1:49 1/5.

Fourteen days later, Fitzsimmons sent Nashua out for one of the smallest, but most significant, purses he had run for since he became a star. The Camden Handicap at Garden State Park was $30,000-added, and the winner's purse was only $22,750, but that was more than enough to elevate Nashua ahead of Citation to become the all-time leading money earner.

Nashua had raced at Garden State only once before, and coincidentally, the Camden was run on May 19, exactly two years since the fledgling had lost the Cherry Hill at the New Jersey track. The Camden was run at one and one-eighth miles. Nashua's weight was

137

back up to his Gulfstream impost of 129 pounds. Fisherman was there again, getting nine pounds, and Mielleux was back, in receipt of nineteen pounds in the field of five. Nashua was 2-5. Arcaro, who had finished eighth in his sentimental Derby run on Head Man, was back aboard, as he would be for the rest of Nashua's races. Nashua again broke in the middle of the pack, but Arcaro hustled him to the front. He led Mielleux by a length or so for six furlongs. When Fisherman came along to be second, Nashua allowed him to stay within a length to about the furlong pole before drawing out handily to win by two lengths in time of 1:49 1/5.

Nashua had then won $1,100,365 to replace Citation as the all-time leading money earner.

Given that his ultimate use for Nashua was as a high-profile stallion, syndicate head Leslie Combs II had decreed at the start of the year that Nashua would not be allowed to carry more than 130 pounds. Coming from a fellow brave enough to orchestrate a syndicate that made a record bid for the horse, this came across as a needlessly meek and carping point of view, which was commented upon in the press rather

freely. (There was no such public pronouncement about Swaps, his foe, but although Swaps carried 130 pounds repeatedly to facile victories, for some reason he was never assigned any more than that weight.)

The announced limit of 130 was first assigned Nashua for the $50,000-added Metropolitan Handicap on May 30, some eleven days after the Camden. Given that he had not shown exceptional dash away from the gate in his races at four, Nashua going a mile around one turn could have been seen at a disadvantage, even under a more modest weight spread. As it was, he was 65-100 in a field of seven, although he was giving away from fourteen to twenty-five pounds.

The Met was an oddly run race. Nashua broke quickly, in second, and dashed to a head lead while dueling Mr. Turf (105 pounds) after a quarter-mile in :22 4/5. There was nothing very judicious about this tactic. After a half-mile, Mr. Turf had taken a daylight lead in :45 1/5, and the oldster still led by a length after six furlongs in a brisk 1:09 4/5. Nashua had dropped to fourth by then, and in the stretch, as Mr. Turf began a fade to last, the 9-1 Midafternoon (111) darted up from last to take command from the ever-present Find

(116). Nashua's accordion-like pattern continued, as he was moved to the rail and rallied, closing a couple of lengths on the pace in the final furlong. Still, he finished only fourth, beaten not quite a length. Switch On (113) wound up second, and Find was third. The time of 1:35 missed Count Fleet's venerated 1942 track record for Belmont by only one-fifth of a second.

While finishing unplaced is usually enough to get some weight off, Nashua's late rally had been noted enough that the weight stayed at 130 pounds for the Carter Handicap at Belmont. This race was run exactly a month later, on June 30. The Carter is an important race, but it is difficult to guess what was seen as the advantage of running in it, for it required Nashua to drop back to a sprint distance, seven furlongs, for the first time since he was two. Also, it came less than a week before one of the key targets for a handicap horse, the one and a quarter-mile Suburban. Since Nashua worked out an extra furlong after the Carter, it might be conjectured that the event was somewhat of a schooling race, but one wonders whether Leslie Combs II would condone such a stratagem with a million-dollar horse he had staked so much of his future upon.

The previous year, the seven-furlong Carter had seen the two crack handicap horses of the moment, High Gun and Helioscope, and both finished off the board. In 1956, Nashua added to that murky distinction. With public confidence sagging, he was still favored, but not odds-on, going off at 6-5. He broke sixth in a field of ten and was not ever really in the race. The race was run at a swift pace, but nothing he had been discomfited by during races in the past (:22 1/5, :45 2/5, 1:10 2/5). Nashua finished seventh, although beaten only about four lengths. He gave sixteen pounds to winner Red Hannigan, 14-1, and up to twenty-two to the others. The time of 1:23 1/5 was one and one-fifth seconds over the remarkably enduring track record of Roseben, set fifty years before. Nashua was caught in 1:38 1/5 for the mile.

However Nashua's supporters might try to explain them, these were two unplaced efforts, and his third such result in his last five races! Was Nashua one of those horses who, with maturity, lose interest?

Fitzsimmons' history was not one to take the tack of ducking the issue, regardless. The market breeder in Combs might have had flickers of announcing

Nashua's retirement, posturing for the public that something had been amiss in his last two races and had just been diagnosed. Nashua would not have stood alone as the only subject of such decision making in racing's annals, but to Combs' credit, the strategy was full speed ahead.

The Suburban Handicap in the year 2000 no longer has the position it enjoyed for much of its century-plus history. In 1956, however, it was still the epitome of the New York handicap scene. Its winners included Salvator, Ben Brush, Beldame, Whisk Broom II, Grey Lag, Crusader (twice), Equipoise, Eight Thirty, Devil Diver, Armed, Assault, and Tom Fool — heroes of eras distant and current. In the 1950s, if you loved New York racing, you conferred upon the Suburban a special reverence.

Nashua suffered an unlucky bit of timing in the race. Despite his two losses, he was still carrying a high weight, 128 pounds, for the one and a quarter-mile fixture. What made the task so difficult, however, was that it coincided with a point in the maturity of a horse named Dedicate who presaged the grand things to come. Indeed, Dedicate was to be the champion older

horse of the next season, when he defeated Bold Ruler and shared honors with him as Horse of the Year. Prior to the 1956 Suburban, however, Mrs. Jan Burke's son of Princequillo, while clearly a nice colt for trainer Carey Winfrey, had not shown championship form. Thus, he got into the Suburban under only 111 pounds. Nashua was giving him seventeen pounds just as Dedicate was ready to announce his entry into the top ranks of older runners.

Dedicate was sent off at 18-1 for the $75,000-added Suburban on Independence Day. Nashua, coming back four days after his embarrassing seventh, was nonetheless still favored, again at 6-5. Metropolitan winner Midafternoon, getting eleven pounds from Nashua, was second choice at 4-1, while Fisherman, now getting thirteen pounds, was not quite 5-1 in a field of eight.

Fitzsimmons resorted again to blinkers for the first time since Nashua's debut at three. Peering through this equipment, Nashua for the first time in several races broke first. He was drawn in post four, and Dedicate was immediately inside him. Jockey Headley Woodhouse sent Dedicate after the champion, and after a quarter-mile in :23 4/5, the two were into a bit of a battle. This was a case of a dangerous front runner with a feathery assignment, and Arcaro was wise to what might happen if he and Nashua were not aggressive enough. After a half-mile in :46 3/5, Dedicate was in front by a head, and Nashua was right there. The rest of the field was already consigned to await the next holiday.

The battle raged and became more daring. Dedicate zipped the next quarter-mile in :23 3/5, and Nashua was right at his throatlatch. Another two furlongs whisked by, and still it was a head-and-head duel. After a mile in 1:35, they swung for home, Dedicate still clinging to the lead.

They had run six furlongs in time two-fifths over the track record and a mile in time one-fifth over the mark. Surely, the pretender would crack. Instead of taking command at that point, however, Nashua actually retreated. At the furlong pole, Dedicate was recorded in the chart to have increased the margin to a half-length. A third consecutive defeat was staring Nashua in the face. Under the whip again, Nashua dug deep. Not only did he recover the lost half-length to draw even, but he then began to power ahead. Closer came the wire;

wider became the big colt's margin. At the finish, Nashua had drawn out enough to win by one and a quarter lengths from the gallant Dedicate.

The time of 2:00 4/5 was only four-fifths of a second over the Belmont Park record, which had been credited to Whisk Broom II since 1913, but had always been suspect of having benefited from inexact chronographs or personnel of his day. Oddly, only two of the last three winners, Tom Fool and Helioscope, each pushed to the limit, had recorded faster Suburbans, both at a single fifth swifter than the 1956 running. Dedicate punctuated his arrival by winning the Brooklyn Handicap soon afterward. The following year, he got his revenge on Arcaro by whipping The Master and Bold Ruler at scale weights in the one and a quarter-mile Woodward.

At year's end, Joe Estes proclaimed the Suburban, "the best race of Nashua's career — or something very close to it."

With things in the Nashua camp righted, he for once followed a spectacular, mini-climax with another victory instead of a downturn. Ten days later, Nashua appeared for the third time in his career in New Jersey.

This time, instead of Garden State, he was performing at the elegant and sumptuous seaside track, Monmouth Park. A crowd of 38,893 greeted him for the $100,000-added Monmouth Handicap.

Going one and a quarter miles again, he was assigned 129 pounds. Although there were seven rivals, the timing of the race, coupled with Nashua's resounding victory in the Suburban, produced the weakest field mustered against him that year. The weight spread, however, still made it a legitimate challenge, for he was giving away a minimum of eighteen pounds to the sterling female runner Manotick and as much as twenty-four to Seven Chances. Receiving twenty-two pounds was none other than Mielleux, who had beaten him to the wire at Gulfstream! Nashua was 3-10, none of the others shorter than 8-1.

The track was muddy, but it was no matter. Nashua broke in the middle of the pack, but Arcaro put him on the lead early and he toured comfortably ahead of an outclassed field. He and Flying Chief prompted each other to a :22 4/5 opening quarter, and then Nashua assumed control. Despite the track conditions, Nashua ran six furlongs in 1:11, at which point he led by four lengths. His ambling mile time of 1:36 4/5 matched Helioscope's track record for the distance, and he still led by four. Through the stretch, Nashua was geared down and galloped home to his easiest victory of the year. He won by three and a half lengths from Mr. First, with Mielleux third. The time was 2:02 4/5, the casual aspect of the final stages allowing him to strut to the wire with a final clocking one and three-fifths seconds slower than the track record.

Waves of applause greeted him. Nashua never won with 130 pounds, but his final handicap, as matters transpired, found him easily triumphant under a single pound less. As Charlie Hatton remarked in *The American Racing Manual*, "He made useful stakes horses look useless."

The Brooklyn Handicap came up three weeks later and was a logical target for a barn-storming handicap horse based in the East. Jimmy Kilroe, who had succeeded the much admired John B. Campbell as racing secretary for New York tracks, was faced with a matter of professional principle. A weight of 130 or less would produce a star for the Jamaica Race Track crowd and management. On recent form, however, Kilroe reckoned Nashua should be weighted at 132 pounds — two pounds above the owner's proclaimed limit. Kilroe, true to his craft, assigned Nashua 132. Combs, true to his word, ducked.

A new race, a $100,000-added handicap at one and one-eighth miles, had been booked at another Jersey seaside track, Atlantic City, for August 11, a week after the Brooklyn. Swaps and the unbeaten European Ribot had each been assigned 130 pounds by a dreaming management. Nashua was pegged at 129 and was the only one headed for the race. At 2:20 p.m. on the afternoon of the Atlantic City Handicap, however, veterinarians were summoned hastily to Nashua's stall at the track. Colic, which had helped truncate his juvenile campaign, had returned, and in a severe form. He was scratched.

The one and a quarter-mile Saratoga Handicap came up two weeks later, on August 25. Although Nashua's colic attack had been strong enough to be termed "violent" in the press, he had recovered so quickly that the Saratoga race was seen as potentially his next target. On August 17, Combs appeared in the Saratoga press box to announce — no doubt feeling some heat — that if, after a work the next day, Mr. Fitz deemed Nashua

ready, the colt would start in the Saratoga Handicap, "regardless of the weight assigned him."

Three days later, however, Nashua got another touch of colic, and although it was less severe than the earlier one, it convinced Sunny Jim that running him on August 25 was not the prudent move. Kilroe again assigned Nashua 132 pounds, and lest this be read as dudgeon, we should add that Kilroe reduced the spread between Nashua and Dedicate from seventeen pounds in the Suburban to nine pounds.

With a number of weeks of interrupted well-being, and training, Nashua did not start again until September 29, in the weight-for-age Woodward Stakes at Belmont Park. This meant that two and a half months, and two colic attacks, had passed since the Monmouth Handicap.

The $75,000-added Woodward, at one and a quarter miles, drew a field of only four, and all were ages four or five, so each carried 126 pounds. The crowd apparently felt Mr. Fitz the magician could overcome all the upheaval and loss of time and made Nashua 3-10. His old rival Jet Action was second choice at almost 4-1, while Mister Gus, trained by Charlie Whittingham for Liz Whitney's Llangollen Farm, had shipped in from the West and was nearly 5-1. Mister Gus had been second to Swaps in three consecutive California races in mid-summer, getting up to nineteen pounds from the rejuvenated Ellsworth sensation.

Over a track rated good, Nashua ran very much as he had in the Sysonby at Belmont a year earlier. He was beaten for the early lead by Jet Action, alternated on the lead with him for most of the race, and was all out to have a half-length on him at the finish. As had been true in the Sysonby, though, both were felled by a strong runner in the stretch, as Mister Gus came along to win by two and a half lengths. The time of 2:03 was three seconds off the Whisk Broom II track mark.

Nashua now had run nine times at four and had won only five. While three of those victories had bespoken a great deal of speed, quality, courage, and the ability to give significant weight to high-class horses over testing distances, it was undeniable that he had failed to dominate as he had in the past. One more race remained, another run in the two-mile Jockey Club Gold Cup.

Jockey Bill Shoemaker's later comments on his suspicion of Swaps' ultimate stamina notwithstanding, there was talk that autumn that the (virtually) all-con-

quering Swaps might turn up for the Gold Cup. After all, by then he had swung from the West through Chicago and was stabled in New Jersey. The Gold Cup was set for October 13, two weeks after the Woodward. Whether Ellsworth and Tenney seriously entertained thoughts of the two-mile race is academic, for on October 9 tragedy struck when Swaps fractured a bone in his right hind leg during a workout at Garden State Park. His very life seemed to hang in the balance. Ironically — but not really so oddly — it was Sunny Jim Fitzsimmons who had a stall sling among his equipment, and he rushed it down to Mesh Tenney to use on Swaps. The Horse of the Year recovered, but, of course, never raced again.

Nashua's final curtain came down on a day of remarkable distinction in American racing. His triumph in a second Jockey Club Gold Cup came in the sixth race at Belmont that day. The seventh was the Futurity, which was won by Arcaro and Fitzsimmons with Wheatley Stable's streaking Nasrullah colt Bold Ruler. It was inevitably seen as a changing of the guard, passing of the baton — choose your cliché.

Nashua did not have an easy time of it in the Gold Cup. A pair of three-year-olds who loved distance ran at him in relays, and one of them, C. T. Chenery's Third Brother, had the temerity to edge ahead after one and a half miles of Nashua and Arcaro being in front. Under the whip, Nashua charged back and once again proved his mettle and his stamina. He would not allow anything less than victory as his exit from the stage. He not only drew away to win by two and a quarter lengths, but did it in 3:20 2/5, a new American record as well as track record for the exalted two-mile distance.

Nashua had been sent off at 3-4 against his erstwhile conqueror Mister Gus, who was at 4-1. Mister Gus chased him in second in the early going, but having gotten a taste of a different Nashua from the previous race, did not keep up and finished fourth, beaten eight lengths. Greentree Stable's Riley was second at 5-1 and Third Brother third at 19-1 in the field of seven. As three-year-olds, the second- and third-place finishers each carried 119 pounds to Nashua's 124 in the weight-for-age event of $50,000-added.

Hatton, as usual, reached for the perfect imagery: "In America's Turf headquarters (Belmont Park)...its trees like huge bouquets, the sun dappling the paddock, bathing the crowd and horses in a soft, golden glow...the setting was something to inspire Sisley. And when the Cup and Futurity had been decided, thoughts like 'the King is dead, long live the King' naturally occurred to everyone present."

Maybe Hatton was no Faulkner, but he surely gave of his best.

Asked if the Gold Cup were Nashua's best race, Mr. Fitz ducked superlatives, perhaps the same as any other veteran of seventy years in one game might: "I wouldn't like to say that. It was a good one, but then he has run so many good ones. As for the time, I don't pay much attention to records."

Nashua had won six of ten races at four and earned $343,150.

He was thus retired with a career mark of twenty-two wins in thirty starts, four seconds, and a third, with an earnings record of $1,288,565. That figure stood as a record for two years, until surpassed by Round Table in the autumn of 1958.

With Bold Ruler, Sunny Jim Fitzsimmons remarkably was entering yet another phase of training a horse that would contend for recognition as his best in an enduring career. The following year, Bold Ruler was the champion three-year-old and shared Horse of the Year with Dedicate. He won the Preakness to give Mr. Fitz his thirteenth Triple Crown race victory, a mark that stood alone as a record for forty-three years — until matched by D. Wayne Lukas with the victory of Commendable in the Belmont Stakes of the year 2000.

At four, Bold Ruler perhaps was even better, although not voted the champion, and he went to stud at Claiborne Farm, where he set a 20th century record by leading the American sire list eight times.

Perhaps out of tact, Fitzsimmons was quoted as saying that, of the horses he trained, Bold Ruler would be best at a mile, Nashua best at one and a quarter miles, and Gallant Fox best at one and a half miles or more.

For his part, Arcaro was surely proud of Nashua's final race. "He was terrific the day he won the Jockey Club Gold Cup," Eddie told his National Press Club audience a few weeks later. "And, in case you're interested, I believe that we could have beaten Swaps in the Gold Cup. There are damned few horses in this country that could beat Nashua going two miles."

Arcaro retired after the 1961 season. He died in 1997.

Incredibly, Sunny Jim Fitzsimmons continued train-

ing long enough to win his final stakes race with a daughter of Bold Ruler. The occasion was the 1963 race named for his old idol from childhood, Miss Woodford, at Monmouth Park. The winner was the three-year-old Bold Ruler filly King's Story, who thus became the 149th individual horse with which Mr. Fitz had won a stakes race. King's Story was a Wheatley Stable homebred.

During Mr. Fitz' retirement, we once dared to sidle hesitantly up to seek a brief and reverent audience. He was seated in a lawn chair near the paddock at Hialeah. Sunny Jim was sharp of mind, and courteous, but one could not help noting that he was so frail as to create the illusion of virtually looking through the skin of his arms. It was the winter after Bold Lad's wonderful juvenile championship for Wheatley Stable, and the question of the day was how would he fare at three. Mr. Fitz had not trained that crop, but he had paid attention. "The one I like for later on is Bold Bidder," he said of another Wheatley Bold Ruler colt.

Mr. Fitz died about a year later, at age ninety-one, in 1966 — the year Bold Bidder was voted America's champion older male.

CHAPTER 8

Patriarch Of The Bluegrass

On the Thursday after Nashua's final victory, he appeared under colors for the last time. The occasion was a farewell exhibition in the leafy autumn of Keeneland Race Course in his new home of Lexington. Alfred Robertson accompanied Nashua on his last voyage, and even Sunny Jim Fitzsimmons and Eddie Arcaro were there with Leslie Combs II to honor the horse in the paddock of the track.

Arcaro was aboard the final time. He galloped Nashua around the track as those in a crowd of some 8,900 mused on when they had last seen him, or perhaps wished that somewhere along the way they had made more of an effort to watch him race. After galloping Nashua around the track, Arcaro let him roll through the stretch, and the colt seem to revel in this last chance to show a crowd his speed. He leveled off and was clocked in :23 for a quarter-mile, "the great diminishing hawk" in one final show of breathtaking arrogance.

The crowd then turned its attention to the sixth race of the day, the sun slowly set on the rolling Bluegrass country, and Nashua was vanned to Spendthrift Farm. He was measured at 16.2 1/4 hands, girthed 73 1/4 inches, and was weighed at 1,090 — calling into question the previously reported 1,200 pounds.

Man o' War stands alone in history as a four-legged attraction to the Bluegrass. Nashua perhaps topped the next echelon, at least until Secretariat's arrival in 1973. For a brief period, he even was under the care of one of the sons of Man o' War's famous groom, Will Harbut. Tom Harbut was one of many of the old gentleman's children to become involved with horses.

Soon enough, however, another eloquent black man, Clem Brooks, became most closely associated with Nashua. It was he who held in thrall the visitors who flocked to the big horse's stall at Spendthrift. Initially, Nashua was housed in a traditional Kentucky frame barn, with pitched roof and glistening white paint. Later, Combs built a modern, squared-off-U barn, which became known as "the Nashua Motel."

Many years later, after Nashua's death at the age of thirty, the importance of the horse lingered to the extent that *The New York Times* published an article over Combs' byline:

What Nashua meant, and will mean, to the Thoroughbred business is a question that is easy to answer. He was one of racing's first big national stars. He was a champion, a fantastic racehorse, but one who had his faults, faults which caused him to lose races when, probably, he shouldn't have lost them. But when he wanted to run, he was almost invincible. Maybe that's what made him so popular; he was "human."

It is also pretty easy to describe what Nashua meant to Spendthrift Farm. He put it on the map. Just as an example, nearly 20,000 people a year used to come to the farm to see Nashua and talk with his groom, Clem Brooks...There have been nearly 300 yearlings by Nashua which were sold at public auction, and a lot of those were instrumental

in making Spendthrift Farm the leading con-
signor eighteen times...in the Keeneland
summer sales.

Not only because of his class, but because
of his age, he became an object of great pride
and affection for all the people who work at
Spendthrift. He just had something that made
people sit up and take notice; I guess today
they would call it charisma.

I've been around a lot of good racehorses
and a lot of good stallions in my life, from
Alibhai and Royal Charger and Jet Pilot to
Majestic Prince...but not one of them meant
as much to me as Nashua.

He meant class and character, but you
never knew what he was going to do next, and
that's probably what made him so exciting.

Nashua was fashionable from the beginning of his
stallion career, but old rival Swaps got off to a faster
start. Swaps' early crops included the champion fillies
Affectionately and Primonetta and the Kentucky
Derby-Belmont winner Chateaugay, along with No
Robbery, Main Swap, and others. Swaps beat Nashua

as the first sire of a yearling to sell for $100,000 or more, and to make matters more ironic, the consignor of that flashy yearling of 1961 was none other than Combs of Spendthrift Farm!

Nashua had no answer for such a concentration of class. Then, however, as Swaps' stud record flagged and never recovered, Nashua churned along, getting a good percentage of sound, rugged stakes winners year after year. By the end of his career, Nashua had become, in Combs' proud words, the "sixth all-time leading sire of stakes winners." Nashua sired a total of seventy-seven stakes winners, or twelve percent. Ten percent, generally, is regarded as exceptional for any stallion.

Swaps first stood at Rex Ellsworth's California ranch for one season before being sent to Darby Dan Farm, then, in another irony, was moved to become Nashua's neighbor at Spendthrift when he was syndicated in 1967. Swaps wound up with thirty-five stakes winners (eight percent). Himself a horse of arresting nobility, Swaps died in 1972.

Nashua never sired the "big horse" in the sense of a son that approached his class, although his Diplomat Way won the Arlington-Washington Futurity when it was the richest race in the world. Diplomat Way added the Blue Grass Stakes in 1967, and many years later, emerged as a top broodmare sire of 1998 when his grandson Skip Away reigned as Horse of the Year. Also, the Nashua colt Noble Nashua put a nice touch on the ironies when he won the major race named the Swaps Stakes in 1981, and he also added the Marlboro Cup as well as several other stakes.

Nashua did, however, sire a concentration of noteworthy fillies. Three of his daughters won the Coaching Club American Oaks. They were Bramalea, Marshua, and Shuvee. Bramalea, as we shall see, was destined to great influence as a producer. It was Shuvee who became the signature runner among Nashua's foals. She swept the 1969 New York Fillies Triple Tiara (Acorn, Mother Goose, and CCA Oaks) and added the Alabama at three, then at four and five was the champion older mare. In both her championship seasons, Shuvee imitated her sire by winning the Jockey Club Gold Cup, and it was still run at two miles in both those runnings, just as it had been for Nashua's pair of victories.

Nashua never led the sire list, but got as close as second in 1964 and ranked in the top five two other years.

As a sire of yearlings, he was highly fashionable for a number of years. His aggregate record, an average of $35,362 for 298 yearlings sold at auction, does not seem impressive today. Nashua, however, sent his first yearlings into the sale ring when the select summer sales average was just over $11,000. It rose to $200,000 during his active career, but most of his key years were tilted toward the low end of that range. His first yearlings, for example, included a $59,000 filly that was tops for her gender at Keeneland in 1959.

As a broodmare sire, Nashua left a legacy whose limits are difficult to imagine. His daughters produced 123 stakes winners. More important than numbers, however, are two specific grandsons. The aforementioned Bramalea, who defeated champion Cicada in the 1962 CCA Oaks, produced the colt Roberto. A son of Hail to Reason, Roberto was bred by John W. Galbreath of Darby Dan Farm and was sent to Europe, where he won the historic Epsom Derby and defeated the otherwise unbeaten Brigadier Gerard in the Benson & Hedges Gold Cup in 1972. Roberto would become so significant a stallion that he is often identified with his own branch of the Turn-to sire line. His

sons who have become major sires in their own right include Brian's Time, Kris S., Silver Hawk, Lear Fan, and Red Ransom. It is appealing to recall that William Woodward Sr. had intended Nashua as his Epsom Derby hope for the crop of 1952. Nashua's grandson Roberto won that race in 1972, and Roberto's son, Silver Hawk, sired the 1997 Epsom Derby winner, Benny the Dip.

Another of Nashua's daughters was the nice stakes winner Gold Digger, who traced to the great Spendthrift family of the mare Myrtlewood. Gold Digger was retained by Combs to race, with the intent of returning her to the Spendthrift broodmare band. In 1971, Gold Digger's handsome yearling by Raise a Native topped the Keeneland summer sale on a bid of $220,000. He was purchased by A. I. Savin and named Mr. Prospector. The colt was trained by Jimmy Croll.

Mr. Prospector flashed prodigious speed, and posted two sprint stakes wins after overcoming a couple of injuries. His prowess as a progenitor was such that he soon earned his way from Florida to Claiborne Farm. He lived to the age of twenty-nine, dying in 1999. Mr. Prospector became the all-time leading sire of stakes winners, with 168 through 1999.

He was a son of the chestnut Raise a Native, so it was easy to think one was seeing plenty of Nashua in the bay Mr. Prospector. The lazily slung ears, which had prevailed in the pedigree since Nashua's broodmare sire, Johnstown, showed up yet again. The head was therefore sometimes judged, perhaps unfairly, to be plain. (Plain horses do not top Keeneland summer sales.) Although Mr. Prospector got his share of unsound runners, there was plenty of Nashua to be detected, too, in his get, be they chestnuts or bays with black points.

In Mr. Prospector, Nashua's blood had many promises to keep. These were fulfilled in the forms of such as Forty Niner, Gulch, Fappiano, Gold Beauty, Seeking the Gold, and their own proliferation of offspring.

When Nashua was twenty-four years old, the Maryland horseman John Williams came to Spendthrift as manager. Williams had a lifelong reverence for the horse and never became blasé about the good fortune of having the grand old man under his care. Williams says today that more than a bit of his own understanding of soundness, bone, and conformation built for action comes from studying every inch of Nashua.

While Combs could articulate in print a certain sentiment, those who work around such a horse develop an even deeper bond. Williams recalls that Nashua as an aging patriarch became a bit unsteady in the act of breeding. Such was the horse's intelligence, understanding, and expectations of his human servants, that he would allow members of the crew to cup their hands under his front heels to give a tiny, but significant, assist. "You don't usually want to be touching the front legs of a horse in the act of covering a mare. It's a good way to get hurt. But Nashua understood — he accepted the help," Williams recalled.

Being around Nashua was not a constant genuflecting before royalty, however. During Williams' tenure, he recalls the great jockey Angel Cordero Jr. visiting the farm and remarking about what a great horse Nashua was, although his career predated Angel's glories. Brownell Combs, the son of Leslie Combs II who later took over management of Spendthrift, was with Cordero.

"Would you like to ride him?" Williams asked Cordero, on a sudden whim. "I gave him a leg up, and Nashua bucked. He didn't wait a moment for Cordero to sit on him. There probably hadn't been anybody on his back since Arcaro, and Nashua bucked instantly. Cordero bailed out and landed on his feet, smiling." Mark up one more victory for Nashua.

A half-dozen years after Williams came to Spendthrift, or in February of 1982, he had an unwelcome truth spelled out for him. Barely a month before, the farm had feted Nashua's thirtieth birthday, and such was the lasting vitality of the stallion that it was planned that he still would serve some mares that year. By February, however, the onset of laminitis was about to cause the sort of pain that need not be tolerated.

Williams, of course, asked and received the permission of Leslie Combs II to have the horse euthanized. As a courtesy of gentleman to gentleman — animal lover to animal lover — he also sought the "permission" of Clem Brooks, "because they were such great friends for all that time." Brooks made himself scarce.

"I couldn't find him. He disappeared," Williams recalls. "He knew what I'd have to say.

"I held the horse while the vet put him down. I cried like a baby. It was one of the saddest days of my life. We had a coffin built to bury him, and we lowered

him down in a bed of straw. We buried Nashua facing the breeding shed."

Liza Todd, the sculptress daughter of Elizabeth Taylor, was commissioned to execute a sculpture of Nashua being led by Clem Brooks. It was later placed in the central yard of the "Nashua Motel."

So, twenty-eight years after "the Segula colt" had stirred the blood of young men and old, the long road had wound to its dead end. The sap had risen only to recede. The victories, the losses, and — yes — even the deaths, had been assigned those permanent places where their differences become less stark, and the pages of the *Racing Form* had yellowed in silence. Eddie Arcaro, though, was one of the many still around and still subject to fall into rapturous memory. The writer Russ Harris invited Arcaro to a horsemen's and horse fan's luncheon around the time of Eddie's eightieth birthday. On that occasion, Harris recalled, Arcaro said that, "If Nashua had Bold Ruler's (free-running) disposition, he would have been the greatest horse that ever lived. On his day, and if he wanted to, Nashua could beat any horse I ever saw."

The Master had spoken.

NASHUA's
PEDIGREE

		Pharos, 1920	Phalaris Scapa Flow
	Nearco, 1935		
		Nogara, 1928	Havresac II Catnip
NASRULLAH (GB), b, 1940			
		Blenheim II, 1927	Blandford Malva
	Mumtaz Begum, 1932		
		Mumtaz Mahal, 1921	The Tetrarch Lady Josephine
NASHUA, bay colt, 1952			
		Jamestown, 1928	St. James Mlle. Dazie
	Johnstown, 1936		
		La France, 1928	Sir Gallahad III Flambette
SEGULA, dk b, 1942			
		Sardanapale, 1911	Prestige Gemma
	Sekhmet, 1929		
		Prosopopee, 1916	Sans Souci Peroraison

NASHUA's RACE RECORD

Nashua — b. c. 1952, by Nasrullah (Nearco)–Segula, by Johnstown — **Lifetime record: 30 22 4 1 $1,288,565**

Own.–Leslie Combs II
Br.– Belair Stud Inc (Ky)
Tr.– J. Fitzsimmons

Date	Cond	Dist	Times	Race	PP	St	1st	2nd	Str	Fin	Jockey	Wt	Odds	Figs	Top finishers	Comment	Field
13Oct56-6Bel	fst	2	:491 2:282 2:541 3:202	3↑ J C Gold Cup 54k	1	1	1½	2hd	11½	12¼	Arcaro E	124wb	*.75	102-09	Nashua1242¼Rily1191¾ThrdBrothr1194	Kept to strong drive	7
29Sep56-7Bel	gd	1¼	:47 1:112 1:371 2:03	3↑ Woodward 80k	1	2	1hd	3nk	31½	22½	Arcaro E	126wb	*.30	82-12	Mister Gus1262½Nashua126½Jet Action12620	No excuse	4
14Jly56-6Mth	my	1¼	:46 1:11 1:364 2:024	3↑ Monmouth H 114k	7	1	14	14	14	13½	Arcaro E	129wb	*.30	92-20	Nashua1293½Mr. First1105Mielleux1071	Speed in reserve	8
4Jly56-7Bel	fst	1¼	:463 1:101 1:35 2:004	3↑ Suburban H 83k	4	2	2hd	2hd	2½	11¼	Arcaro E	128wb	*1.20	96-10	Nashua1281¼Dedicat1112¼Subhdr1125	Well rated,going away	8
30Jun56-7Bel	fst	7f	:221 :452 1:102 1:231	3↑ Carter H 58k	3	6	44½	65	62¾	73½	Arcaro E	130 w	*1.10	90-12	Red Hannigan1141½Switch On119½Artismo111¾	Well up,hung	10
30May56-7Bel	fst	1	:224 :451 1:094 1:35	3↑ Metropolitan H 55k	7	1	32½	42½	53	4¾	Arcaro E	130 w	*.65	98-09	Midaftrnoon111hdSwtchOn113½Fnd116nk	Came again too late	7
19May56-7GS	fst	1⅛	:463 1:111 1:362 1:491	3↑ Camden H 33k	4	1	11	1½	11	12	Arcaro E	129 w	*.40	91-10	Nashua1292Fisherman1201½Mielleux1102	Very handy score	5
5May56-7Jam	fst	1⅛	:49 1:13 1:38 1:503	3↑ Grey Lag H 55k	6	3	2hd	1hd	1hd	1hd	Atkinson T	128 w	*.95	93-17	Nashua128hdFind118hdFisherman1201¾	Almost fell at start	7
17Mar56-8GP	fst	1¼	:47 1:113 1:36 2:003	3↑ Gulf Park H 112k	6	5	43½	53¼	56	57	Arcaro E	129 w	*.70	89-08	Sailor1191¾Mielleux1101Find116¾	Wide both turns,tired	7
18Feb56-8Hia	fst	1¼	:463 1:104 1:353 2:02	3↑ Widener H 129k	9	3	41¾	2½	2hd	1hd	Arcaro E	127 w	*.40	95-11	Nashua127hdSocilOutcst121hdSlor119nk	Under strong drive	9
Previously owned by Belair Stud																	
15Oct55-6Bel	sly	2	:494 2:321 2:583 3:244	3↑ J C Gold Cup 79k	3	2	1½	11	13½	15	Arcaro E	119 w	*.25	80-14	Nashua1195Thinking Cap11915Mark's Puzzle1198	Easy score	5
24Sep55-6Bel	sly	1⅛	:451 1:101 1:36 1:491	3↑ Sysonby 106k	5	1	41½	3nk	22	31¾	Arcaro E	121 w	*.65	91-10	HighGun126hdJetActn1261¾Nshu1213½	Weakened when urged	5
31Aug55-7Was	gd	1¼	:46 1:102 1:373 2:041	WP Match 100k	1	1	1½	11½	12	16½	Arcaro E	126 w	1.20	81-17	Nashua1266½Swaps126	Drew far out to handy score	2
16Jly55-7AP	fst	1	:231 :453 1:093 1:351	Arl Classic 148k	2	2	22	24	21	1½	Arcaro E	126 w	*.30	96-10	Nashua126½Traffic Judge1201¼Impromptu1204	Under a drive	7
2Jly55-0Aqu	fst	1¼	:493 1:134 1:382 2:034	Dwyer 55k	3	1	1½	11½	11½	15	Arcaro E	126 w	-	88-15	Nashua1265Saratoga12240Mainlander114	Easing up late	3
Run as special event with no wagering																	
11Jun55-6Bel	fst	1½	:49 1:133 2:042 2:29	Belmont 119k	5	2	1hd	12½	16	19	Arcaro E	126 w	*.15	93-12	Nashua1269Blazing Count1265½Portersville1266	A romp	8
Geldings not eligible																	
28May55-7Pim	fst	1 3/16	:471 1:11 1:353 1:543	Preakness 116k	5	4	42½	2hd	1hd	11	Arcaro E	126 w	*.30	106-08	Nashua1261Saratoga1267TrafficJudg126nk	Rated,mild drive	8
7May55-7CD	fst	1¼	:472 1:122 1:37 2:014	Ky Derby 152k	5	3	31	2½	2½	21½	Arcaro E	126 w	*1.30	96-12	Swaps1261½Nashua1266½Summer Tan1264	Good bid,no excuse	10
23Apr55-6Jam	fst	1⅛	:471 1:111 1:363 1:503	Wood Memorial 111k	4	2	21½	22	21½	1nk	Atkinson T	126 w	1.10	93-17	Nashua126nkSummer Tan12625Simmy1266	Sensational score	5
26Mar55-7GP	sly	1⅛	:463 1:122 1:391 1:531	Fla Derby 148k	1	5	56½	22½	2½	1nk	Arcaro E	122 w	*.95	78-26	Nashua122nkBlueLem1132¼FirstCabin1131	Unruly,hard urged	9
26Feb55-7Hia	fst	1⅛	:462 1:113 1:371 1:493	Flamingo 141k	2	2	1hd	1hd	1hd	11½	Arcaro E	122 w	*.70	88-12	Nashua1221½Saratoga1224½CupMan1227	Drifted out in drive	12
21Feb55-0Hia	fst	1 1/16	:231 :47 1:114 1:441	Alw 7500	2	2	3nk	2hd	1½	11½	Arcaro E	126wb	-	94-11	Nshua1261½Munchausen1172HappyMemries1142½	Unruly late	4
Special event run between 2nd and 3rd races - No wagering																	
9Oct54-6Bel	fst	6½f-W	:222 :451 1:092 1:153	Futurity 112k	6	4		21	1½	1hd	Arcaro E	122wb	*.65	94-06	Nshua122hdSummrTan122¾RoylCoinage1227	Held on gamely	7
Geldings not eligible																	
1Oct54-6Bel	fst	6f-WC	:22 :442 1:081	Sp Wt 10000	4	2		4¾	2hd	11	Arcaro E	118wb	*1.05	100-00	Nashua1181Royal Coinage1185Pyrenees1181½	Clever score	7
21Sep54-6Aqu	fst	6½f	:223 :451 1:092 1:16	Cowdin 30k	9	1	2hd	4¾	41½	21½	Arcaro E	124wb	*1.25	101-12	SummerTn1201½Nshua124¾Bunny'sBabe1201½	Mildly impeded	10
28Aug54-6Sar	fst	6½f	:23 :464 1:111 1:174	Hopeful 78k	4	1	1½	1hd	11	1nk	Arcaro E	122wb	*.55e	96-18	Nashua122nkSummrTan1221½Pyrens1221½	Well rated,held on	8
21Aug54-4Sar	fst	6f	:23 :463 :592 1:122	Grand Union Hotel 27k	5	2	23	1hd	12	11¾	Arcaro E	122 w	2.75e	86-17	Nashua1221¾Pyrens1152½ModlAc1143½	Won in clever fashion	6
19May54-7GS	fst	5f	:221 :454 :583	Cherry Hill 20k	3	5	2½	22	21½	2nk	Higley J	119 w	3.80	98-13	RoyalNote122nkNashua1195Menolen1191½	Unruly all the way	11
12May54-6Bel	fst	5f-WC	:221 :453 :58	Juvenile 15k	1	2		1hd	2½	1½	Arcaro E	117 w	3.00e	89-18	Nshua117½SummerTn1228Lugh1172	Scored under clever ride	8
5May54-4Bel	fst	4½f-W	:222 :462 :523	©Md Sp Wt	14	9		81½	11½	13	Higley J	118 w	8.50e	86-14	Nashua1183Retract118½Danger Quest118no	Won in hand	21

Index

Photo Credits

Cover photo: (The Blood-Horse)

Page 1: Nashua with Eddie Arcaro (The Blood-Horse); Nashua head shot (The Blood-Horse)

Page 2: Nasrullah (Meadors Photo); Nearco (British Racehorse); Segula (Bert Morgan); Johnstown (Caufield & Shook, Inc.)

Page 3: William Woodward Sr. (Bert and Richard Morgan); Nashua with William Woodward Jr. (Belmont Park); Belair Stud (J. A. Estes)

Page 4: Leslie Combs II and Sunny Jim Fitzsimmons (The Blood-Horse); Ted Atkinson (Bert Morgan)

Page 5: Nashua in Saratoga winner's circle (The Blood-Horse); Winning the Hopeful (Saratoga Photo); Winning the Futurity (Bert Morgan)

Page 6: Winning the Florida Derby (Jim Raftery/Turfotos); Winning the Wood Memorial (Bert Morgan)

Page 7: Swaps winning the Kentucky Derby (Courier-Journal and Louisville Times); Nashua winning the Preakness (Baltimore Sun); Winning the Belmont Stakes (Belmont Park)

Page 8-9: Nashua-Swaps Match Race (Keeneland-Morgan); Match Race winner's circle (The Blood-Horse); Nashua winning the Jockey Club Gold Cup (Bert Morgan)

Page 10: Winning the Suburban (Bert Morgan); Winning the Grey Lag (The Blood-Horse); Winning the Widener (Hialeah Photo)

Page 11: Winning the 1956 Gold Cup (Bert Morgan); Nashua and Al Robertson (Bert and Richard Morgan)

Page 12: Nashua leaving Belmont (United Press Photo); Nashua and his connections at Keeneland farewell ceremony (both The Blood-Horse)

Page 13: Noble Nashua (The Blood-Horse); Diplomat Way (The Blood-Horse); Shuvee (Bob Coglianese)

Page 14: Mr. Prospector (Turfotos); Gold Digger (The Blood-Horse); Roberto (Alec Russell); Bramalea (Bob Coglianese)

Page 15: Nashua and the author (Courtesy Ed Bowen); Spendthrift main house (Anne M. Eberhardt); Spendthrift sign (Barbara D. Livingston); Nashua grazing (Charles Rippy)

Page 16: Nashua conformation (The Blood-Horse); Statue (Anne M. Eberhardt)

About the

Author

E dward L. Bowen is considered one of Thoroughbred racing's most insightful and erudite writers. A native of West Virginia, Bowen grew up in South Florida where he became enamored of racing while watching televised stakes from Hialeah.

Bowen entered journalism school at the University of Florida in 1960, then transferred to the University of Kentucky in 1963 so he could work as a writer for *The Blood-Horse*, the leading weekly Thoroughbred magazine. From 1968-70, he served as editor of *The Canadian Horse*, then returned to *The Blood-Horse* as managing editor. He rose to the position of editor-in-chief before leaving the publication in 1993.

Bowen is president of the Grayson-Jockey Club Research Foundation, which raises funds for equine research. In addition to *Nashua*, Bowen has written ten books, including *Man o' War* and *Dynasties: Great Thoroughbred Stallions*. Bowen has won the Eclipse Award for magazine writing and other writing awards. He lives in Lexington, Ky., with his wife, Ruthie, and five-year-old son George. Bowen has two grown daughters, Tracy Bowen and Jennifer Schafhauser, and one grandchild.

Forthcoming titles
in the

THOROUGHBRED
Legends®

series:

Spectacular Bid

John Henry

Personal Ensign

Sunday Silence

Available titles

Man o' War

Dr. Fager

Citation

Go for Wand

Seattle Slew

Forego

Native Dancer

www.thoroughbredlegends.com

Editor — Jacqueline Duke
Assistant editors — Judy L. Marchman, Rena Baer
Book design — Brian Turner